Lansdale, Magsaysay, America, and the Philippines

A Case Study of Limited Intervention Counterinsurgency

Andrew E. Lembke, Major, US Army

B.S., United States Military Academy, West Point, New York,
2001

Fort Leavenworth, Kansas

2012-02

Abstract

Historians tend to agree that Ramon Magsaysay's leadership and his relationship with Edward Lansdale are two of the most important features of the Philippine governments campaign against the Huks from 1946-1954. Yet the nuances of his leadership and the nature of their relationship deserve greater investigation. This thesis seeks to further illuminate Magsaysay and Lansdale's relationship by focusing on the role of empathy and sociocultural understanding, in defeating the Huks and restoring the Philippine government's legitimacy. US policy in the Philippines at the time, bolstered regimes riddled with corruption, graft, and nepotism, reinforcing poor governance, and resulting in a loss of government legitimacy. This energized the Huk movement until they were on the verge of toppling the government. A change in US policy coincided with the emergence of Magsaysay and Lansdale. They reversed Huk momentum, rejuvenated the demoralized and oppressive armed forces, and restored the Philippine government's legitimacy, all in less than four years. Their shared, genuine empathy for the Filipino people fostered deep sociocultural understanding. Their combined capabilities and resources then translated empathy and sociocultural understanding into concrete measures to combat the Huks and rebuild popular support for the government.

Acknowledgments

I would like to thank first and foremost my wife Lachlyn for her support and encouragement throughout this process, despite our geographic separation. She has, without fail, pushed me to complete my work based on her own notable academic accomplishments. She has truly been one of my most important guides.

The support of my thesis committee, consisting of Dr. D. Scott Stephenson, Dr. Joseph Fischer, and Dr. Nicholas Murray, was absolutely essential to the successful completion of my thesis. Their feedback and insights have proven invaluable throughout the course of this endeavor, and without their support I have no doubt that my work would have fallen short of the mark.

During my research in the Philippines I received the utmost support of the US Embassy team in Manila. Ambassador Harry K. Thomas and his staff, headed by Executive Secretary Ms. Eloisa Williard, were instrumental in arranging a number of my interviews with Filipino notables. Within the embassy team I would also like to specifically thank Mr. Ramon Taruc for coordinating my interview with his distant relative, Dr. Romeo Taruc.

In addition to the support of the US Embassy team I would like to acknowledge the assistance of another group that was extremely supportive of my efforts in the Philippines. The West Point Association of Graduates of Manila, specifically Ms. Grace Jarque and Captain Mark Posadas (Philippine Army, West Point Class of 2004), proved invaluable in facilitating my research. I would also like to acknowledge Mr. Jim Cisek (US Embassy Manila, West Point Class of 1974) for introducing me to this wonderful community.

I am eternally grateful to Dr. Daniel Marston. If it were not for his advocacy I would not have had this opportunity. I would also like to thank him for his editorial advice and assistance. Other academics I would like to acknowledge are Dr. Douglas Macdonald and Colonel (ret.) Joseph Felter. Dr. Macdonald, currently a Visiting Research Professor of National Security Affairs at the Strategic Studies Institute, was kind enough to review my early thesis ideas and help me focus them on the topic I finally settled on. Colonel (ret.) Felter, currently a Research Fellow at the Hoover Institution at Stanford University, provided invaluable assistance in facilitating my research at the Hoover Institution Archives, as well as my research in the Philippines.

I would be remiss in not thanking the subjects of my research in the Philippines. I am truly indebted to former President Fidel V. Ramos, former senator Ramon Magsaysay, Jr., Mr. Alfredo Lim, mayor of Manila, Dr. Romeo Taruc, Municipal Councilor of Angeles City, Pampanga, Mr. Frisco San Juan, president of the Nationalist Peoples Coalition, and Father Jack Schumacher, retired Jesuit priest, historian, and professor at Ateneo University, Manila. Interviews with these men not only shed light on the character and personality of the subjects of my research, but also provided invaluable context for the rest of my writing and research.

I would also like the staffs of the Hoover Institution Archives, the Truman Library, and the Combined Arms Research Library. Their professionalism, dedication, and inherent knowledge after decades of service to their organizations, made them indispensable assets during my limited duration visits. Without their assistance I would not have been able to achieve the breadth of research I finally achieved.

Finally, I would like to acknowledge and thank my fellow Art of War scholars, Will Harris, Lou Ruscetta, and Stephen Campbell. The intellectual rigor they subjected me to on a daily basis constantly challenged me to improve. They were both a source of inspiration and frustration, and were essential to the development of my argument.

Table of Contents

Acronyms

AFP	Armed Forces of the Philippines
AMT	*Aguman ding Malding Talapagobra* (General Workers Party)
BCT	Battalion Combat Team
CIA	Central Intelligence Agency
CIC	Counterintelligence Corps
EDCOR	Economic Development Corps
HMB	*Hukbong Mapagpalaya ng Bayan* (People's Liberation Army)
JUSMAG	Joint United States Military Advisory Group
KPMP	*Kalipunang Pambansa ng mga Magsasaka sa Pilipinas* (National Society of Peasants in the Philippines)
MPC	Military Police Command
NAMFREL	National Movement for Free Elections
OPC	Office of Policy Coordination
OSS	Office of Strategic Services
PC	Philippine Constabulary
PCAC	Presidential Complaints and Action Commission
PHILRYCOM	Philippines Ryukus Command
PKP	*Partido Komunistang Pilipina* (Philippine Communist Party)
USAFFE	United States Armed Forces Far East

Chapter 1
Introduction

The Huk campaign was a classic example of counterinsurgency, with lessons all too often overlooked or misunderstood by those who face the problems of insurgency in other countries of the world.

> — Major General Edward Lansdale, personal correspondence with Lavinia Hanson (Valeriano), 5 March 1984.[1]

American interest in counterinsurgency seems to emerge only when confronted by insurgency. Major General Lansdale's comment in 1984 about the lack of interest in the Huk campaign, and counterinsurgency in general, was likely attributable to a number of factors, among them America's recent experience in Vietnam. The US military focused on the conventional Soviet threat rather than lessons from irregular conflicts. However, since 9/11 the US engaged in two conflicts that developed into counterinsurgencies, and the Huk campaign continued to receive scant attention. Whatever the reasons for previous inattention during the last decade, the Huk campaign bears important lessons for US military and civilian policy-makers.

US defense and foreign policy seems to be shying away from large-scale counterinsurgency operations and nation-building.[2] Yet, if the US intends to defend its national interests abroad it must be prepared to confront the possibility of engaging in future counterinsurgency campaigns. Memories of Vietnam and recent experiences in Afghanistan and Iraq may bias American understanding of counterinsurgency as inherently large-scale, i.e. long, resource and manpower intensive, and generally American-led. Generalizing the characteristics of counterinsurgency in this way ignores both the historical context of the respective situations in Vietnam, Afghanistan, and Iraq, and other examples of successful, small-scale counterinsurgency campaigns. By contrast, US assistance to the Philippine government against the Huks, from 1946-54 provides an excellent case study of limited, yet successful intervention.[3]

The US and Philippine governments were ultimately successful in a counterinsurgency campaign that went poorly for the first four years. The initial years following World War II saw a dangerous mix of ill-informed US policy in the Philippines and a Philippine government beset with corruption and scandal. By 1950 a change in US policy acknowledged the gravity of the situation by tying economic and military aid to political and social reforms.[4] Yet this top-down approach was insufficient to address the most immediate problem. The Filipino masses had lost faith in their government, weakening its legitimacy. Without immediate action to reverse this trend the Huk movement, which was really just a symptom of this loss of faith, stood a very real chance of toppling the government. Essentially, the US approach required a complementary bottom-up approach to tie the people back to their government while the longer term top-down reforms took effect.

Such a complementary approach to national level reform efforts had to rebuild popular faith in and support for the government, thereby reestablishing its legitimacy. Developing the necessary bottom-up strategy required individuals cognizant of the nuances of Philippine politics, and capable of understanding and identifying with the Filipino people. Additionally, the Americans needed a strong Filipino counterpart capable of rallying the people just as they were nearing physical and moral exhaustion. Amidst this need came Edward Lansdale from the US government and Ramon Magsaysay from the Philippine government.

Magsaysay and Lansdale's close contact with and understanding of the people's needs, their unique backgrounds, and common character combined to make them an extremely powerful and effective team, despite their relatively junior positions at the beginning of the Huk campaign. This thesis will argue the collaboration between Ramon Magsaysay and Edward Lansdale emerged as a critical factor in the Philippine government's successful campaign against the Huk movement, from 1946-54, because of their shared empathy for the Filipino people, deep sociocultural understanding, and complimentary capabilities and resources. While this may suggest that it is impossible to duplicate the success of the Huk campaign because of the unique characters involved, it may be possible to replicate the factors of success by finding leaders with the attributes demonstrated by Lansdale and Magsaysay.

The Role of Empathy

This paper will argue that genuine empathy for the Filipino masses was a key feature of the Lansdale-Magsaysay dynamic. In order to analyze and assess the implications of empathy within the context of this case study, and because this is not a paper on leadership theory, a working definition of empathy is required. Dr. Jaepil Choi, in his paper on charismatic leadership, identified the characteristic of empathy as:

> the ability to understand another person's motives, values, and emotions . . . and it involves entering the other person's perspectives . . . sensitivity to followers' needs . . . individualized

attention to followers . . . encourag[ing] personal development . . . [and] displaying support for the efforts of followers.[5]

For the purpose of this paper, empathy is "the ability to experience and relate to the thoughts, emotions, or experience of others."[6] Using this definition and the characteristics of empathy described above, it is clear that this trait is intensely personal; requiring a significant degree of understanding of and contact with subordinates, or in this case the Filipino populace.

Empathy, of all character traits, was a requirement for the efforts of the Philippine and US governments in the campaign against the Huks because of the nature of the conflict. Philippine society, particularly those areas most affected by the Huk rebellion, existed under a paternalistic system whereby the landlords and elites acted as the benefactors or protectors of their patrons and the lower classes.[7] A study conducted by the Center for Creative Leadership notes that "paternalism characterizes leader-subordinate relationships, where a leader will assume the role of a parent and feel obligated to provide support and protection to their subordinates under their care" and that "empathic emotion plays an important role in creating this paternalistic climate of support and protection."[8] The problem for the Philippine and US governments in the mid-1940s was that the Huk seemed to have a monopoly on identification with the Filipino masses.

The Philippine and US governments were combatting an enemy whose main propaganda messages resonated with a popular base that had grown further and further from the landlord and elite class, even before the Japanese invaded in 1941. As will be discussed in more depth in the next section, the divide between rich and poor had increased with time, and the effects of the war and Japanese occupation only exacerbated and accelerated the divide. The Huks offered an appealing narrative that was difficult for the government to counter or deny. They also had a legitimate record of fighting oppression during the occupation that earned the masses' trust. In order to reverse the trend, the masses needed government officials and institutions they could trust. This trust could only be built through genuine empathy for the lower classes plight, and understanding of the ills plaguing society.

Sociocultural Understanding

Forty years of US colonial rule over the Philippines left American officials with an abundance of institutional knowledge of *pre-war* Philippine society and culture. However, the effects of the war and Japanese occupation on Philippine society cannot be overemphasized. In the immediate post-war period the US and Philippine governments adopted policies that failed to acknowledge societal dislocation brought on by the war and in some cases attempted to actively counter a potentially beneficial status quo change.[9] Finally, both governments failed to fully grasp the second and third order effects of Philippine independence on society. In the aftermath of these failures the American and Philippine governments needed individuals capable of understanding *post-war* Philippine society in order to mend the rift between the government and the masses.

Unfortunately, senior US officials in Manila were either holdovers from the pre-war US High Commission in the Philippines, or were imported from elsewhere in Asia, specifically China. High Commissioner, and later ambassador, Paul McNutt "recruited from all the old China hands and all the old Philippine colonial hands."[10] While this should have represented continuity and institutional understanding of the Philippines, these individuals represented a return to pre-war Philippine society. Almost five years after the war, a US government report would note the lost opportunity to rebuild an economically independent Philippines, and avoid a return to the status quo ante after World War II.[11]

The war exposed many of the ills plaguing Philippine society and resulted in a significant degree of dislocation. As will be discussed in greater detail in the next chapter, most of the landlords and elites who could have represented the leadership of Central Luzon fled to the cities and collaborated with Japanese occupation forces. Pre-war peasant and labor leaders stepped into the void, raising local guerrilla groups, eventually coalescing into the Hukbalahap guerrillas in March 1942.[12] Largely due to their origins the Huks remained autonomous from the US directed guerrilla groups in the Philippines, often bringing the two entities into conflict, and fostering a sense of American abandonment during the occupation.[13] Without positive elite involvement in Central Luzon, and with little US involvement, the Huks gained increasing control over the region.

Societal dislocation in Central Luzon manifested itself in a potential change in the social status quo. Where the elites and Americans had provided leadership, governance, security, and social support prior to the war, the Huks filled those roles during the war. With liberation in 1945 the Huks and their peasant supporters felt a justifiable sense of entitlement. The Americans acknowledged the Huks as the most active and aggressive of the guerrilla organizations in the Philippines.[14] They were also arguably the most organized. The Huks believed they deserved recognition and a place in the post-war government. Those aspirations ran counter to both the US and Philippine government's desire for a return to the pre-war status quo.[15]

Finally, both governments failed to realize what Philippine independence meant to the Huks and their peasant base. It should have represented empowerment, acknowledging the status quo change in Central Luzon induced by the occupation's effects. Instead it reinforced a return to the status quo ante, and a return to power of the same men the Huks fought against during the occupation. Thus, for the Huks and their supporters, independence signaled a continuation of the struggle against a government that looked strikingly similar to the collaborationist government.[16] Independence also provided the elites a mandate to destroy the peasant movement in Central Luzon, ensuring the perpetuation of the old social system.

Understanding the dynamics of post-war Philippine society was absolutely essential for anyone to determine proper courses of action to combat the Huks and rebuild popular faith in the government. It was not simply understanding the Huks militarily, as their base of support stemmed from legitimate social grievances. Developing an effective strategy required an understanding of the character of the Huks, the problems facing the people, and the deficiencies of the Philippine government.

Complementary Capabilities and Resources

The Philippine government may have represented one of the biggest obstacles to a successful counterinsurgency strategy. Any strategy that advocated a change in the status quo represented a threat to the Philippine elite establishment. Due to the pervasive political patronage system defining Philippine politics, the status quo represented stability and financial security to elements within business, government, and the military.[17] Anyone advocating a strategy of change needed significant protection and support from the highest levels of the US government as well as widespread popular support from the Philippine masses in order to prevail over the entrenched establishment.

The bottom-up US campaign in the Philippines required unity of effort. The US mission in the Philippines possessed both an ambassador and a general officer in charge of the military assistance mission.[18] Both individuals could potentially claim responsibility for the counterinsurgency strategy. Complicating matters were the parallel chains of command in Washington, DC in both Departments of State and Defense. In order to develop unity of effort, those charged with developing and implementing the strategy had to be capable of garnering the support, confidence, and trust of the US diplomatic and military leadership in the Philippines and Washington.

Support from Washington was also necessary as a transferable commodity to associated Filipino partners. Perceived threats to the establishment would inevitably result in attempts to purge the threats from the government. An individual understood or believed to possess Washington's support had long been a powerful political tool in Manila.[19] Preventing such establishment interference was essential to success. In addition to Washington's support, those Filipino partners also required popular support, which could serve as a counterbalance to the power of the entrenched political and elite establishment. The establishment would find it particularly difficult to get rid of an extremely popular figure.[20]

In adopting a strategy requiring popular support, the US clearly needed a strong Filipino counterpart. However, this person could not be a puppet or merely an expedient tool.[21] The severity of the situation by 1950 required an individual capable of both winning popular support away from a movement that already enjoyed widespread support, while surviving attacks from the entrenched, elite establishment. US support might thwart initial Philippine government attempts to rid itself of a "change agent," but that support would be useless if their counterpart proved untrustworthy to the people. Therefore, the US counterpart had to be genuine and trustworthy, with the force of personality to overcome both the Huks and the entrenched establishment.

The US counterinsurgency effort in the Philippines necessitated a significant degree of trust. Trust on the part of officials in Washington for their personnel in the Philippines, and trust on the part of the masses in their own officials and government. The former could be given; the latter had to be earned, yet both required individuals worthy of that trust. Trust was also essential because of the international situation. Events elsewhere in the world caused an oscillation of US focus on the Philippines. During the war, US military and economic interests saw the post-war Philippines as the "gateway" to Asia.[22] However, post-war Europe almost monopolized US attention until 1949, when China fell to the communists. Even when US attention returned to Asia, the Korean War dominated that attention.[23] Washington's limited focus on the Philippines thus necessitated a significant degree of trust between US officials in Washington and Manila.

This paper will analyze the efforts of Ramon Magsaysay and Edward Lansdale during the Huk campaign, through mid-1954, focusing on the importance of their shared empathy for the Filipino people, sociocultural understanding, and complimentary capabilities and resources. Understanding the need for the unique characteristics found in Magsaysay and Lansdale necessitates understanding the origins of the conflict, and how and why that conflict was able to expand disproportionate to Huk strength. Following this contextual material is a chronological analysis of the situation in the Philippines in the context of Lansdale and Magsaysay's characteristics. Each chapter will analyze a particular phase of the Huk campaign, which in itself became the backdrop of a more troubling struggle for the Philippine government's legitimacy.

Notes

1. Lansdale to Lavinia Hanson (Valeriano), personal correspondence, 5 March 1984, (Lansdale Papers, Box 15, Hoover Institution Archives, Stanford University, Palo Alto, CA).

2. US Department of Defense, *Sustaining US Global Leadership: Priorities for 21ˢᵗ Century Defense* (Washington, DC: Government Printing Office, January 2012).

3. For a general history of the Huk rebellion and the events leading to it, see chapters 11 and 12 of Stanley Karnow, *In Our Image: America's Empire in the Philippines* (New York: Ballantine Books, 1989). For a comprehensive study of the Huks, their origins, and their grievances, see Benedict J. Kerkvliet, *The Huk Rebellion: A Study of Peasant Revolt in the Philippines* (New York: Rowan & Littlefield Publishers, 2002). Edward Lansdale's autobiography, *In the Midst of Wars: An American's Mission to Southeast Asia* (New York: Harper and Row, 1972), and biography by Cecil B. Currey, *Edward Lansdale: The Unquiet American* (Washington, DC: Brassey's, 1998), chronicle Lansdale's activities in the Philippines.

4. Douglas J. Macdonald, *Adventures in Chaos: American Intervention for Reform in the Third World* (Cambridge: Harvard University Press, 1992), 135.

5. Jaepil Choi, "A Motivational Theory of Charismatic Leadership: Envisioning, Empathy, and Empowerment," *Journal of Leadership and Organizational Studies* 13, no. 1 (2006): 27.

6. William A. Gentry, Todd J. Webber, and Golnaz Sadri, *Empathy in the Workplace: A Tool for Effective Leadership* (Greensboro: Center for Creative Leadership, 2010), 3.

7. Benedict J. Kerkvliet, *The Huk Rebellion: A Study of Peasant Revolt in the Philippines* (New York: Rowan & Littlefield Publishers, 2002), 6-7.

8. Gentry, Webber, and Sadri, 6.

9. Upon liberation, the Philippine Islands reverted to its pre-war US commonwealth status. US High Commissioner Paul McNutt served in a caretaker role until Philippine independence on 4 July 1946. While US specialists and experts served as advisors to many Philippine government officials, an indigenous civil service existed, and Filipinos administered the provinces, districts, and villages. The High Commissioner's mission seemed to represent a conflict of interests. While McNutt was supposed to assist the Philippine government in developing policies and legislation facilitating the country's transition to independence, he also represented US policy interests. In such a position, McNutt was able to influence future Philippine domestic and economic policy to America's benefit.

10. Clarence A. Boonstra, Agricultural Officer, Manila (1945-1947); interviewed by Donald Barnes (1989) and Allan Mustard, W. Garth Thorburn,

and James E. Ross (2006), transcript, Oral History Country Reader Series, Philippines, Association for Diplomatic Studies and Training, http://adst.org/oral-history/country-reader-series/. From here on, interviews from the Association for Diplomatic Studies and Training, Country Reader Series, will be cited by the acronym ADST/CRS. Transcripts of all further interviews from ADST/CRS are consolidated at the same internet address.

11. Economic Survey Mission to the Philippines, *Report to the President of the United States by the Economic Survey Mission to the Philippines* (Washington, DC: Government Printing Office, 1950), 12. From here on this source will be cited only as Economic Survey Mission.

12. Luis Taruc, *Born of the People* (New York: International Publishers, 1953), 65.

13. Taruc, 72-73.

14. W. T. T. Ward, 13th Air Force Historical Office, *The Guerrilla Resistance Movement in Central Luzon, About Oct. 26 1944, as Reported to Allied Forces About to Invade the Philippine Islands* (Edward Geary Lansdale Papers, Box 15, Hoover Institution Archives, Stanford University, Palo Alto, CA), 9,

15. Kerkvliet, 117.

16. Taruc, *Born of the People*, 230.

17. Mina Roces, "Kinship Politics in Post-War Philippines: The Lopez Family, 1945-1989," *Modern Asian Studies* 34, no. 1 (February 2000), 182.

18. Thomas B. Buell, *The Quiet Warrior: A Biography of Admiral Raymond A. Spruance* (Annapolis, MD: Naval Institute Press, 1987), 445.

19. Stanley Karnow, *In Our Image: America's Empire in the Philippines* (New York: Ballantine Books, 1989), 630. Google e-book.

20. Carlos P. Romulo, Marvin M. Gray, *The Magsaysay Story* (New York: The John Day Company, 1956), 154.

21. Buell, 446-447.

22. Karnow, 633.

23. Karnow, 633-636.

Chapter 2
Context of a Crisis

Men joined for complex reasons, including severe economic dislocation, starvation, and misery as well as greed and local factionalism. Old grudges and wanton violence could be hidden under a patriotic mantle.

— David J. Steinberg, "An Ambiguous Legacy: Years at War in the Philippines."[1]

Suggesting that Ramon Magsaysay and Edward Lansdale were successful against the Huks for the reasons outlined in the previous chapter implies members of both the Philippine and US governments lacked those qualities. Taken at face value this would seem counterintuitive. Naturally, the Philippine government was comprised of Filipinos and one would think they empathized with and understood their own people. The United States ruled over the Philippines for four decades, and should have had a fairly nuanced understanding of Filipino society and culture. How is it possible that both governments were so ill prepared or unwilling to handle the task of combatting the Huk movement?

The origins of the two government's problems in handling the Huks stemmed from the war and its immediate aftermath. In the case of the Philippine government, the problem lay in their changing society and the development of Philippine democracy. Though class and social divisions existed long before the emergence of the Huk movement, by 1946 these divisions had grown to a point where conflict was almost unavoidable. Exacerbating this division was a political system that favored the few while failing to represent the many.[2] The status quo may have remained for some time, but the outbreak of war in 1941, and the Filipino experience under Japanese occupation, brought the long simmering conflict to a head. These factors all contributed not only to a lack of true understanding of the nature of the problem by the Philippine government, but also discouraged the changes necessary to deal with the problem.

American officials responsible for Philippine policy suffered from a series of overlapping issues. First was misplaced trust in four decades of institutional knowledge of the Philippines that really only amounted to theoretical or superficial understanding. Regarding the Huks, the US based their assessment of the problem and potential solutions on the reports and interactions of groups that were decidedly biased against the movement. The Americans may have overcome these first two issues immediately following liberation. However, US government and military personnel lacked the type of contact with the Philippine populace necessary to develop deeper understanding of the problem, and even if they had the necessary contact, in many cases post-war US officials represented the entrenched local establishment. Additionally, the Philippines represented the center piece of US post-war decolonization policy in the region. America could not be seen interfering in Philippine domestic matters. Underpinning all of these issues, and informing all US actions in the Philippines at the time, was the threat of communism.

War and Occupation

The war and occupation led to the evolution of the Huk insurgency from a localized problem to a national crisis. First and foremost, and perhaps the most obvious point from this period, is the creation of the Huks as an organized movement with a large support base. Next, those Filipinos who collaborated with the Japanese, particularly the elite and land owning class, served as a focal point for Huk and peasant animosity and retaliation during the Japanese occupation, unleashing a cycle of post-war violence that would come close to toppling the Philippine government. Finally, US interaction with the Huks during the war, compounded by their close relationship with the elite and land owning class, colored American policy towards, and understanding of the Huks for the first half of the campaign.

The Huk movement was a manifestation of a wider evolutionary movement, and was not truly revolutionary, despite its much publicized communist leadership. Prior to the war, the 1930s saw three localized peasant uprisings originating from deplorable social conditions. The last of these, the Sakdal rebellion in 1935, saw six thousand peasants engage in widespread attacks on villages and government buildings in provinces south of Luzon, causing significant alarm within the Philippine Commonwealth government.[3] Social unrest was a common occurrence in the agricultural areas of Luzon and the uprisings demonstrated that the will for action was there, but the peasants needed organization and direction.

During the same period, the Philippine Socialist Party developed a strong peasant following under the leadership of men like Pedro Abad Santos, and Luis Taruc, appealing to the same social discord that fueled the uprisings.[4] The Philippine Communist Party (*Partido Komunistang Pilipina* or PKP) of the 1930s was a fairly weak organization with a small support base, having been outlawed by the Commonwealth government, and lacking a narrative that resonated with the average Filipino.[5] When the two parties merged in 1938, retaining the PKP title rather than the socialist title, communist influence increased but still remained weak.[6] The communists still lacked a narrative or common threat that could garner sufficient popular support to achieve their objectives. The Japanese and collaborationist Filipinos would provide the common threat.

The Hukbalahap (*Hukbong Bayan Laban sa mga Hapon* or People's Anti-Japanese Army) was an armed resistance movement established by the United Front on 29 March 1942.[7] The Huk would grow to become "one of the largest and most powerful guerrilla organizations in central Luzon."[8] The PKP exercised varying degrees of control over the local leadership of the organization during the occupation – largely because so many of the senior Huk leaders were also leaders within the PKP – but the rank-and-file consisted of peasants with little to no communist indoctrination. A fairly distinct separation persisted between the Huk movement and the PKP throughout the occupation.[9]

On 27 March 1942, two days before the official formation of the Huks, their supreme military commander Luis Taruc, sent a letter to General MacArthur pledging allegiance to both the US and Philippine governments, and requesting guidance and support, neither of which was forthcoming.[10] In the absence of guidance from MacArthur, and in a desire to maintain autonomy from other US-led guerrilla units, the Huks initiated an aggressive campaign against Japanese forces and the collaborationist government.

The Huks are alleged to have killed 25,000 people in the Philippines during the occupation; of that number only 5,000 were Japanese.[11] These figures are usually used to suggest a reign of terror throughout Central Luzon and as another reason for the US government not formally recognizing the Huks as guerrillas after the war. Regardless of the actual statistics, they must be taken in context.[12] The Huks had a much broader conception of what classified collaborationist activities justifying a death sentence. If the Huks were indeed responsible for the deaths of 20,000 Filipinos, they likely saw the majority of those deaths as justifiable. Throughout Luis Taruc's memoir, *Born of the People*, he recounts Huk activities against Filipino collaborators, but also devotes considerable efforts to describing the positive Huk relationship with the peasants. Therefore, a Huk reign of terror is relative to who was providing the Americans with accounts of Huk activities.

In addition to their military activities, the Huks established local shadow governments that provided peasant conflict resolution, performed civil functions such as marriages, and provided law and order.[13] When liberation forces entered Central Luzon, they found functioning Huk governments in a number of provinces and towns.[14] The Huks governed their relations with the populace and their everyday actions and operations through two pamphlets, "The Fundamental Spirit" and "The Iron Discipline." Taken together these essentially represented the Huk Code of Conduct.[15] Huk public relations did not necessarily transcend class however, with those landlords still present in the provinces targeted as potential sources of weapons, money, and supplies. The landlords that chose to flee to the cities saw their lands seized for use by the Huks and the peasants.

The situation in Central Luzon during the Japanese occupation was nothing less than chaotic. Though the Huks strictly governed their own ranks, as mentioned above, Taruc admits that there were elements within the movement that engaged in unacceptable behavior, such as theft and murder.[16] However, even the American leadership of the United States Army Forces Far East (USAFFE) guerrilla units acknowledged that their own Filipino personnel used the chaos of the occupation to settle old scores and rivalries.[17]

The Americans described the Huks as owing no allegiance to any side in the conflict and constituted a threat not only to the Japanese, but also to USAFFE guerrillas and their intelligence nets.[18] Based on the accounts of former USAFFE guerrilla leaders there may have been good reason for this mistrust. Luis Taruc asserted in his memoirs that USAFFE units actively worked with the collaborationist Philippine Constabulary (PC) to fight the Huks during the occupation.[19] By Huk logic this was tantamount to collaborating with the Japanese. The USAFFE leadership viewed the ill-disciplined PC as vulnerable to infiltration and influence and did on occasion use the PC to fight the Huks in Luzon.[20] With the arrival of liberation forces, the Huks were viewed as an enemy by the Japanese, the landlords and elites, and the USAFFE guerrillas. The latter two groups, particularly the collaborationists, would play a significant role in both US and Philippine government Huk policies following liberation.

It is clear that the Huks publicly offered their services and allegiance to the US and Philippine governments prior to the Japanese invasion.[21] But beyond infrequent contact, the USAFFE-Huk relationship can almost be characterized as a tragic comedy. On numerous occasions the two sides attempted meetings that were either broken up or ambushed by Japanese and collaborationist PC forces.[22] These types of occurrences only fueled suspicion and hostility between the groups and prevented the development of a unified guerrilla command in the Philippines in the early stages of the campaign.[23]

Collaboration was not a new phenomenon in the Philippines. The land owning class that developed under Spanish rule collaborated with the US during the Spanish-American War and the subsequent Philippine Insurrection less than fifty years earlier. There was a certain degree of pragmatism on the part of the landowners and elites in dealing with the Japanese; there was significant money to be made in supplying the occupiers. Also, had they sided with the insurgency they would have potentially legitimized peasant demands for reform following the war. For others, collaboration was an order from the government-in-exile, as a number of prominent post-war politicians claimed.[24] Still others claimed that it was their national duty, that by serving in the "puppet government" they could more effectively protect the Filipino people from within the system.[25] Yet collaboration was no small affair for the elites, with thirty percent of the Philippine House of Representatives, seventy-five percent of the Senate, most of the Supreme Court, and eighty percent of the officers of the Army accepting positions in the collaborationist government.[26]

The people of Central Luzon did not necessarily agree with the logic of the collaborationists. During the occupation, many of the peasants and guerrillas felt that the collaborationist government and associated security forces were more brutal than the Japanese. [27] Significant animosity developed between landlords and elites represented within the collaborationist government, and the rural based insurgency. As one US Army officer serving with the USAFFE guerrilla forces in Central Luzon noted, the region was easily comparable to Hobbes' State of Nature, and the life of the average Filipino civilian reduced to being "nasty, brutish, and short."[28]

The elite and land owning class were not the only collaborators targeted by the Huks. When the US military and fledgling Philippine Army were defeated by the Japanese, the PC largely remained intact. The new rulers and their allies in the collaborationist government quickly set the PC to work, attacking the Huks and their support base.[29] The poorly trained, equipped, and led Constabulary forces resorted to brutality to compensate for their deficiencies. The PC excesses generated hatred within both the Huks and the civilian population that would survive the war and significantly influence the actions of both Huk and PC veterans.[30]

The problem for the Americans started soon after the fall of Corregidor. The USAFFE guerrilla organizations that sprang up throughout the Islands more closely resembled a loose confederation of organizations than a single united front. While various USAFFE unit leaders attempted to convince the Huks to submit to USAFFE command, the Huks resisted. Huk commander

Luis Taruc noted a general arrogance and disdain for the Huks within the US guerrilla leadership.[31] Captain Ray Hunt, a former USAFFE guerrilla confirms the disdain, but not for Taruc's perceived reasons. The American guerrilla leaders were all traditional, conventional US Army officers with no background in and little regard for guerrilla warfare, viewing it as a necessary evil.[32] Ironically, while the Huks generally viewed the USAFFE guerrillas more as bandits and militarily ineffective, several USAFFE veterans grudgingly acknowledged Huk military prowess.[33]

The USAFFE guerrillas, loosely directed by MacArthur's headquarters, were also disdained by the Huks for their lack of activity. Ironically, the PKP advocated a defensive policy that would have brought the Huks more in line with USAFFE policy.[34] However, for the peasants of Central Luzon there were few alternatives to armed resistance. Many landowners used the occupation as an opportunity to crush the peasant movement in Central Luzon. The lawlessness of the period, combined with Japanese support for the elites meant there were few limitations to the depredations in Central Luzon during the occupation. Had the Huks agreed with the PKP leadership, they might have found common ground with the USAFFE guerrillas to establish a united front against the Japanese.

Another problem for the Americans in the Philippines during the occupation was actually in Brisbane, Australia, the location of General MacArthur's headquarters. In May 1943, MacArthur chose Colonel Courtney Whitney as his chief of the Philippine Regional Section within the Allied Intelligence Bureau. The official history of intelligence operations in the Philippines during the war cites Whitney's selection as derived from a need to "place in charge an individual having a very broad knowledge of the Islands and the personalities involved."[35] Unfortunately, Whitney was quite possibly one of the worst choices for a job that included coordination of intelligence and guerrilla activities in the Philippines, described later as "undiplomatic, belligerent...[and] condescending toward all Filipinos, except those, who like himself had substantial investments in the islands."[36] The man General MacArthur relied on the most to lay the groundwork for post-liberation Philippine policy firmly believed in a return to the status quo ante, though events after liberation demonstrated that he was not the only one with this view.[37]

As the occupation ended and liberation began, American understanding of the Huks came from two main sources. The first source was the negative interaction between USAFFE guerrilla units and the Huks, and the second was information provided by the collaborationist elites favored by American senior leadership.[38] Ironically, the same Philippine collaborationists who provided information about the Huks would later use American assessments of the guerrillas derived from that information, in determining official guerrilla recognition in the post-war years.[39] Poor American understanding of, and Philippine elite hostility towards the Huks ensured a short honeymoon between the three parties as liberation gave way to tentative peace. America's institutional knowledge of the Philippines not only proved shallow, it failed to account for the devastating effects of the war.

The Aftermath: 1945-1946

The war decimated the Philippine economy. A pre-independence assessment by United States Army Forces Western Pacific intelligence staff painted a rather discouraging picture, stating that it "was far worse than what was envisioned in 1941," and went on to provide the following summary:

> Property damage alone is estimated between $700 and $800 million. The Philippine government faces probable expenditures of ₱186 million for its first fiscal year, with an estimated income of only ₱6 million . . . Foreign trade is too scant to sustain the Philippine economy as formerly. The cost of living has risen to 6-1/2 times the pre-war level, while the 1945-46 food crop is 30% below normal. Many necessities of life are nearly impossible to obtain except through the black market . . . in Manila alone, there was 70% damage to housing . . . Nearly 80% of the schools need to be rebuilt. Only 40% of the pre-war power plants are operating today.[40]

In this uphill economic battle another significant issue hindered the Philippines, the structure of the Philippine economy under US sovereignty.

As US business interests found a ready market for consumer goods in the Philippines, as well as an abundant source of raw materials and commodities, the local economy developed to meet the demand. The development was unbalanced at best. US interests focused on raw material and commodity extraction rather than developing locally based industry and manufacturing. Indigenously manufactured consumer goods were unnecessary in the Philippines because US goods were readily available for import. The economic imbalance fostered dependence, and was incentivized by an absence of tariffs between the Philippines and the United States.[41]

In a 1946 cable to the State Department, US High Commissioner to the Philippines, and later ambassador, Paul McNutt explained the economic situation. From 1909 to 1941 trade relations between the United States and the Philippines encouraged economic dependence. Interests in the Philippines saw where the money lay in regards to exports and adjusted their production and focus accordingly. The proposed economic transition period was originally scheduled from 1941-46 in a move to extricate the Philippines from this economic dependence. The transition failed to materialize due to the war, and with independence looming the Philippine economy faced collapse because it would no longer enjoy the preferential treatment it had prior to independence.[42] While the landlords and elites would survive the economic transition associated with independence, the lower classes would experience the greatest upheaval.

Deplorable economic conditions only exacerbated an already growing problem in the post-war Philippines. Despite President Roosevelt's strong stance on collaboration his death opened the door to a more liberal policy advocated by General MacArthur and other key members of his staff.[43] The death of Philippine Commonwealth president-in-exile Manuel Quezon during the war, brought Vice President Sergio Osmeña to power. Osmeña was politically weak within the Nationalista Party, and so sought the support of other groups outside of the party by taking a hard line on the collaboration issue. Osmeña was soon opposed by Manuel Roxas, a senior official within the collaborationist government, member of the Philippine establishment, and long-time friend of General MacArthur.[44]

Through a series of deft political and legal moves, Roxas was able to declaw all of Osmeña's attempts to push the collaboration issue.[45] These efforts proved successful in garnering Roxas significant support from collaborators within the government and security forces when he split from the Nationalista Party and formed the Liberal Party for his presidential bid against Osmeña. In a close race Roxas defeated Osmeña and assumed the presidency, promptly pardoning all collaborators not already held and indicted by American forces. In one swift action Roxas put an end to the collaboration issue, much to the outrage of former Huks.[46] While the historical record clearly demonstrates Roxas' actions and intent being motivated by self-interest, the period from the first American amphibious landings in the Philippines until the end of the war are far from clear.

The months encompassing the American liberation of the Philippines represents an example of historical "he-said-she-said" between the Huks and their opponents, and is unlikely to ever be fully resolved. Former USAFFE guerrilla leader, Captain Ray C. Hunt aptly notes in his memoirs that there were four reasons why it is unlikely anyone will ever produce an accurate history of the entire guerrilla campaign: 1) most of the key figures are dead; 2) many leaders never kept diaries or records; 3) internecine rivalry between various group leaders generated biased accounts following the war, particularly those about specific individuals; and 4) towards the conclusion of the campaign when US-Philippine success was clear, countless people attempted to join the guerrillas or later claim they had been one, in order to reap post-war rewards.[47]

However, from existing accounts from both the USAFFE guerrillas and the Huks it is clear that the Huks had already experienced the beginnings of retribution long before Manuel Roxas took up residence in the presidential palace at Malacañan. The Americans clearly viewed the Huks as a threat, disarming Huk squadrons – at gunpoint in some instances – during the course of liberation.[48] In an extreme case, a disarmed Huk squadron of more than one hundred men was detained by a USAFF- recognized unit in Malolos, Pampanga Province and summarily executed. The leader of the unit was quickly arrested by the Americans and then quickly released and appointed mayor of Malolos.[49] Huk leaders, including Luis Taruc, were quickly arrested and held by the US Counterintelligence Corps (CIC), in some cases multiple times, but eventually released.[50] The rapid expansion of communism in the post-war world made US officials wary of groups even remotely communist, and the Huk leadership fit the description.[51]

The Americans also contributed to the growing problem through the officials chosen to rebuild the diplomatic corps in the Philippines. The US mission in the newly liberated country closely resembled the US mission before the war:

> All MacArthur's friends and all McNutt's prewar colonial administration friends were there, and they had reinstalled the old elite crowd, the old rulers, the old colonial rulers of the Philippines, who all wanted the sugar industry and the prewar structure done.[52]

While it might seem appropriate to have rebuilt the diplomatic corps with experienced personnel who were familiar with the Philippines, those personnel simply reinforced a return to the status quo ante. They lacked interaction with the lower classes, remaining focused on their limited contacts within the upper classes. Even when an outsider, Senator Millard Tydings arrived in the Philippines to assess the situation and develop rehabilitation aid recommendations MacArthur confined his survey to Manila, preventing the congressman from seeing the situation in Central Luzon and elsewhere.[53] The almost willful ignorance of US officials regarding the growing social conflict in the immediate post-war period contributed to almost five years of ill-informed Philippine policy.

As the status quo returned to Central Luzon following liberation, the landlords built up private armed groups that came to be popularly referred to as Civilian Guards. Hired from amongst the ranks of the former collaborationist PC, these paramilitary forces were often paid and equipped by the government.[54] In addition to pay and equipment the Civilian Guards acted as auxiliaries for the most recent manifestation of the PC, the Military Police Command (MPC), as the landlords attempted to reassert control over Central Luzon.[55] It is this period that suffers the most from a plethora of contrasting, and at times contradictory stories about who was at fault for the greatest amount of violence. However, while specific, verifiable accounts are difficult to come by, multiple sources on both sides refer to the general lack of discipline and training, and the widespread abuses of the MPC and Civilian Guards from their inception through 1949.[56]

Under the guise of a "pacification program" the MPC and Civilian Guards increased the frequency and intensity of their operations prior to and during the April 1946 congressional elections.[57] In response, Hukbalahap veterans started banding together to resist the increased attacks by the MPC and Civilian Guards, and the violence in Central Luzon escalated.[58] At the same time, PKP and former Huk leaders and the Roxas administration were attempting to negotiate a peaceful settlement. As previously mentioned, both sides were guilty of armed violence while each accused the other of having started it.[59] The Huks had tentatively disbanded after the war, and local violence was not coordinated and remained localized. However, by June 1946 former Huk senior leaders met to discuss a "contingency plan" to prepare for possible hostilities against the government, resulting in the formation of the *Hukbong Mapagpalaya ng Bayan* (People's Liberation Army), or HMB.[60]

Complicating matters was US policy that seemed schizophrenic at best, hypocritical at worst. The growth of nationalism, reinforced by the exploits of wartime resistance movements and Mao's successes in China, had a ready appeal in Southeast Asia with the conclusion of the war. When the Dutch attempted to reassert their control over the Dutch East Indies they found a well-entrenched Indonesian independence movement ready to fight for their sovereignty.[61] Ho Chi Minh's Viet Minh forces in Indochina had already declared a republic and initiated hostilities toward Chinese nationalist and Indian Army forces by the time the French returned.[62] Meanwhile, Filipino nationalist sentiment was strong, but found an outlet in the independence promised by the United States in 1946.

Philippine independence was the centerpiece of US anti-colonial policy in Asia. President Truman was pushing his European allies to grant independence to their colonial possessions, and desired that Philippine independence represent the first step towards greater self-determination in post-war Asia.[63] In so doing, the US would be able to effectively counter Soviet propaganda, and potentially increase the number of pro-Western/pro-democracy members of the new United Nations Organization. Taken together, these factors were rapidly making the emergence of a democratic, economically viable, and stable Philippines a "no fail" mission.[64]

Following the Japanese surrender in September 1945, 50,000 US troops remained in the Philippines to take part in this "no fail" mission. This number would rapidly decrease as the US downsized its military forces generally, and was forced to commit troops to occupation duties in Europe and elsewhere in Asia.[65] In addition to being committed to the defense of the Philippine Islands against external aggression, the US government realized the importance of maintaining a presence in the Islands as a base of operations against potential communist aggression in the Far East. However, the size and disposition of those forces remained a point of debate and contention up to and beyond Philippine independence on 4 July 1946.[66] American defense concerns were not the only factor influencing the situation in the Philippines in the aftermath of the war.

Despite a defense policy that supported Philippine independence, the US economic policy designed to rebuild the Philippines resembled a return to the status quo ante, including continued Philippine dependence on the United States.[67] The influence of US business interests was manifested in the Bell Trade Act of 1946. Secretary of State James F. Byrnes was critical of the provisions of the bill that showed favoritism towards American economic and development interests and believed that it was counter to America's stated goals in the Far East.[68] The United States government tied ratification of the Bell Trade Act in the Philippine Congress to US rehabilitation aid, a move of questionable integrity that political scientist, Dr. Douglas Macdonald describes as "a most ungenerous treatment of a battered ally."[69] Philippine economic devastation represented a perverse opportunity in that it offered an almost blank slate to retool the economy towards self-sufficiency and relative economic independence.

Ratification of the Bell Trade Act became an important issue in the Philippines in 1946. The Philippine press quickly grasped the ramifications of the bill and excoriated it in editorials throughout 1946.[70] The controversy surrounding the bill increased the importance of the 1946 congressional elections for President Roxas and the Liberal Party. They needed three-fourths majority in both houses of congress in order to pass an amendment to the Philippine Constitution for the Bell Trade Act's "parity rights" clause, granting US citizens full commercial rights equal to those of Filipino citizens.[71] The elections did not result as Roxas wished. Six candidates from the Democratic Alliance ticket, which included PKP and former Huk members, were elected to congress that April. The six men, Luis Taruc among them, were decidedly against the Act and their votes would prevent ratification.[72]

In a move that undermined the Philippine government's legitimacy, Roxas had the six Democratic Alliance congressmen, and five other opponents of the Act, unseated from congress citing their alleged use of violence and intimidation to win their seats.[73] However, all six Democratic Alliance men came from provinces in Central Luzon where the MPC and Civilian Guards were active throughout the April 1946 election, but had won large majority victories. Besides Roxas' clear motivations for the move, a Liberal Party congressman may have accurately identified a further reason for unseating the Democratic Alliance congressman, essentially observing that they do not represent the interests of elite class.[74]

The war was the catalyst for the conflict between the Philippine government and the Huks. In the absence of contact with or guidance from the government in exile, the Huks instituted what amounted to shadow governments in the barrios, districts, and provinces. After decades of attempting to gain political legitimacy the Huks experienced nominal independence and authority in Central Luzon during the occupation. Much to their delight, Huk authority came at the expense of the landlords and elites who were generally in support of the Japanese. Huk military forces gained significant experience fighting the Japanese and collaborationist Philippine government forces and viewed themselves as a proper guerrilla army. Essentially, during the occupation they succeeded in temporarily altering the status quo in their favor. The US supported return to the status quo ante and subsequent Philippine government actions against the Huks represented a point of no return as both sides hurtled toward open conflict.[75]

Missed Opportunities: 1946-1949

The period following Philippine Independence on 4 July 1946, can best be characterized as a series of missed opportunities. Reconstruction and rehabilitation of the Philippines lagged far behind what should have been accomplished given the hundreds of millions of dollars in aid provided by the US government. The Philippine government also missed the opportunity to repair the relationship between the government and elites and the lower classes of society. Another significant missed opportunity was the reinvigoration of Philippine representative democracy. While President Roxas' controversial actions surrounding the unseated congressmen in 1946 represented a setback for representative democracy, the 1949 presidential elections dealt a significant blwo to popular faith in the government. Finally, the Philippine government missed the chance to deal a decisive blow to the PKP and Huks when they were at their weakest.

Events elsewhere in the world distracted officials in Washington from the developing crisis in the Philippines.[76] As the Department of State Philippine Desk Officer recalled, "I had been called by Dean Acheson and told that, "I've got a lot of things to do, a lot of things on my mind. You're on the Philippine desk now. You go ahead and decide what has to be done."[77] Communism was on the march in Europe and other parts of Asia. Communists were leading civil wars in Greece and China, communist republics had been declared in Albania and Bulgaria, and Soviet forces continued to occupy much of Eastern Europe. Additionally, US policy towards the Philippines necessitated minimal intervention. Yet US policy was inadvertently supporting a Philippine government trend towards authoritarianism which was undermining popular government legitimacy.[78]

The post-war Philippines return to the status quo truly got into full swing following the passage of the Bell Trade Act. As rehabilitation aid and war damage claims money flowed in, the elites quickly set to work rebuilding the same pre-war industries that ensured Philippine economic dependence on the United States.[79] While this move could possibly be explained away as simple short sightedness on the part of the elites, after the industries were rebuilt and functioning, rather than reinvesting profits in research and development, and increasing production capacity, substantial sums were instead invested in commerce and trade. In the aftermath of the war with so few industries operating, demand for imports was extremely high making trade and commerce extremely lucrative.[80] Substantial profits served to perpetuate a cycle that prevented the development of industries that could provide locally produced products to replace imported products.

As elites remained profit focused, their counterparts in government routinely prioritized projects and programs benefitting the upper class. Projects and programs designed to alleviate the conditions of the lower classes were given lower priority. Schools, hospitals, and public projects received significantly less governmental attention than did the critical pre-war industries of sugar mills, saw mills, and mines.[81] While industry was critical to rejuvenating the Philippine economy, the public works sector deteriorated so badly during those years that teachers almost annually went without pay for up to three to four months.[82] Despite large expenditures for residential construction in the Philippines, particularly in Manila, there was virtually no change in living conditions for the lower classes. The lack of improvement for the lower classes suggests most of the funds, some of them public funds, went towards construction in only upper class areas.[83]

In the three years following independence little was done to alleviate the situation of the average Filipino. In this case, as previously, responsibility rested with the upper class of Philippine society. As recovery got underway, 1947-1949 saw inordinately large profits on the part of wealthy landowners and businessmen, while wages remained extremely low.[84] Despite the windfall profits of the wealthy, the tax burden remained largely on the lower classes. The vast majority of the government's tax revenue came from excise and sales taxes while a correspondingly small percentage of revenue came from taxes likely to effect the wealthy.[85] By simply raising wages – one of the Huk demands – and reforming the tax code to evenly distribute the burden, the government and elites might have gone a long way towards mending class and social divisions.

Compounding the economic disparity between the elites and landowners were the abuses of the Civilian Guards and MPC. The observations of the Civilian Guards and MPC noted previously not only continued, they worsened as the brutality of these group's retaliations increased. Discipline and training had not improved, but their firepower had, and Civilian Guard and MPC frustration at increasingly effective Huk attacks and a recalcitrant populace was manifested in widespread destruction.[86] Several congressmen and provincial officials publicly protested against MPC abuses in their provinces.[87] As a contemporary *Manila Times* editorial noted:

> These practices, and other depredations by official and quasi-official forces, have created the feeling among people that the Huks somehow embody social virtue while the government and its people are capable only of brutal excesses. This is the kind of feeling from which governments fall.[88]

Nevertheless, the landlords and elites were reasserting their authority in the provinces militarily, opting out of a negotiated peace that risked reforms.

The destruction advocated and authorized by elites was part of President Roxas' "mailed fist" campaign.[89] Ironically, this campaign ostensibly started as a peace initiative. Both President Roxas and President Elpidio Quirino, who succeeded Roxas following is sudden death in 1948, offered amnesty to the Huks. However, both sides refused to back down from certain key demands. The Huks understandably refused to give up their arms until the Civilian Guards were abolished and MPC attacks halted. The government insisted on disarmament before negotiation.[90] When the Huks rebuffed Roxas and then Quirino, both men insisted they had tried every approach to peace and their only recourse was the armed destruction of the Huks and their supporters.[91]

The Philippine government faced a crisis of legitimacy. Abuses by the government's representatives in uniform, the MPC, and their paramilitary proxies, led the people to believe that officials in Manila did not truly represent them. After all, why would a government of the people send its soldiers to fight the people? It was no coincidence that as the government was losing popular support, the Huks were gaining it. Luis Taruc believed that "the Huks can only hold out as long as it is supported by the masses. No more, no less."[92] Part of this belief likely stemmed from a lack of external support from other communist countries.[93] External support has become a commonly accepted and major factor in successful subversive insurgencies.[94] Lacking external support the Huks had to rely entirely on popular support, further emphasizing how suicidal the Philippine government's actions toward its own people must have appeared.

The final failure was in rebuilding popular faith in the government. Luis Taruc, like many Filipinos and others within the Huk movement, grew up learning US history in the American run schools of his youth. Taruc counted among his heroes many of the American founding fathers, and was capable of reciting the Gettysburg Address well into old age.[95] He had certain expectations of and ideas about democracy, fueled in no small part by his admiration for the democratic ideals learned decades earlier. Philippine independence held special meaning for many of the Huks and their support base. It represented an opportunity for change, but the events of 1946 severely damaged their belief that they could achieve change through the Filipino version of democracy. Unfortunately the events of 1949, largely attributed to President Quirino and his Liberal Party, would eclipse those of 1946.

The general election of 1949 was widely acknowledged as beset by widespread corruption and violence. A senior member of the Philippine Electoral Commission observed "there is no more democracy in the Philippines."[96] As a friend who ran in the congressional elections in 1949 would later joke with Edward Lansdale, he received only one vote in the entire district, and with his own vote cast for himself, he was sure that at least his mother had voted for him.[97] A non-Huk led uprising broke out in Batangas Province, south of Manila because of the corruption.[98] The AFP and PC, at the direction of political masters, assisted in the fraud. Local police forces operated "generally as the goons and pluguglies of the local political bosses."[99] The election also resulted in a new Huk slogan, "bullets not ballots."[100] This simple slogan encapsulated the effect that Quirino's administration had on the Philippines by 1949; representative democracy was an illusion and the only way to break free of government oppression was through violence.

The 1949 election reinvigorated the Huk movement by providing them with a popular and undeniable narrative about the government's irretrievable state. Prior to the elections the Huks were struggling to find mass appeal outside of Central Luzon, and discipline was beginning to break down.[101] Additionally, the PKP continued to oppose armed struggle in favor or parliamentary struggle, and focused on developing the "urban working class" until mid-1948, when they finally rejoined the Huk movement.[102] From 1946 to 1948, armed opposition in Central Luzon went largely uncoordinated and should have made an easy target for a multi-pronged government approach that combined military operations with reforms. Yet the elections resuscitated the movement, and before long they would pose an existential threat not just to Philippine stability, but to the government itself.[103]

By the close of 1949 the Philippine government had squandered hundreds of millions of dollars, with US consent, rebuilding a pre-war economy not suited to economic independence. Under the Quirino administration income and social inequality increased, and popular faith in the government was virtually destroyed, thus undermining its legitimacy. As the government neared economic collapse because of failed policies, the armed forces were steadily getting worse, and were operating within an increasingly hostile populace. Amidst this chaos the Huks were getting stronger. Even without the realignment of the PKP and HMB in 1948 and the resulting improvement in organization, the Quirino administration was pushing more and more peasants and urban sympathizers into the Huk camp.[104] The outlook for the Philippine government was grim as 1950 dawned.

Notes

1. David J. Steinberg, "An Ambiguous Legacy: Years at War in the Philippines," *Pacific Affairs* 45, No. 2 (Summer, 1972): 182.

2. Economic Survey Mission, 2-3.

3. David R. Sturtevant, "Sakdalism and Philippine Radicalism," *The Journal of Asian Studies* 21, no. 2 (February 1962): 208. See also, Kerkvliet, 37.

4. Taruc, *Born of the People*, 33.

5. Kerkvliet, 50-58.

6. Kerkvliet, 50, 264-266. See also, Taruc, *Born of the People*, 46.

7. Taruc, *Born of the People*, 65. The United Front consisted of the AMT, or General Workers' Union, a Pampanga based organization, and the KPMP, or National Society of Peasants in the Philippines. The AMT and KPMP were a mix of social and labor movements organized to represent peasant and labor demands.

8. Ward, 9.

9. Taruc, *Born of the People*, 66. See also, Kerkvliet, 102-104; Ray C. Hunt, Norling, Bernard, *Behind Japanese Lines: An American Guerrilla in the Philippines* (Lexington, KY: University of Kentucky Press, 1986), 105. Google e-book.

10. A copy of the original letter was provided by Dr. Romeo Taruc during an interview with the author on 18 October 2012, Angeles City, Pampanga. For a short biographical sketch of Dr. Taruc see Appendix C.

11. Edward G. Lansdale, "A Comparison: Viet Nam and the Philippines" (Lansdale Papers, Box 74, Hoover Institution Archives, Stanford University, Palo Alto, CA), 6,

12. For a map of the main Huk areas of operation see Appendix A.

13. Taruc, *Born of the People*, 124, 179.

14. Kerkvliet, 108-109.

15. Taruc, *Born of the People*, 67.

16. Taruc, 128-129.

17. Hunt, Norling, 105; See also, Michael Guardia, *American Guerrilla, the Forgotten Heroics of Russell W. Volkmann* (Havertown, PA: Casemate Publishers, 2010), 113. Google e-book.

18. Ward, 9.

19. Taruc, *Born of the People*, 149.

20. Hunt, Norling, 106-107.

21. Taruc, *Born of the People*, 52. While there is ample evidence of the Huk's proclamations of support for both the US and the Philippine government-in-exile, it is difficult to ascertain their sincerity. US and Philippine government sources believed that the Huks never intended to really support the government, and were using the occupation as an excuse to arm and prepare. The Huks can claim that US officials offered little tangible support or acceptable guidance, forcing them to take their own path.

22. Taruc, *Born of the People*, 148, 159. See also Hunt, Norling, 106.

23. Sources from both USAFFE and the Huk Movement note that both sides believed in the concept of a unified command structure that would coordinate all guerrilla activities in the Philippines, but USAFFE insisted that the Huks subordinate themselves to the American led organization. The Huks steadfastly refused this demand. For the general USAFFE opinion on unified command see Hunt, 103. For the Huk opinion on unified command see Taruc, *Born of the People*, 155-156.

24. Karnow, 628-629. See also, William Manchester, *American Caesar: Douglas MacArthur 1880-1964* (New York: Hachette Book Group, 1978), 375-376. Google e-book.

25. Claro M. Recto, *Three Years of Enemy Occupation: The Issue of Political Collaboration in the Philippines* (Manila: People's Publishers, 1946), 74; See also, Manchester, 376; Hunt, Norling, 154.

26. Bernard Seeman, Salisbury, Laurence, *Cross-currents in the Philippines* (New York: Institute of Pacific Relations, 1946), 22. Further references to an "elite and land owning class," or derivations thereof, should not be mistaken as a generalization that all elites or landowners acted the same or held the same beliefs about the Huks and peasantry. Philippine society was far too complex to make such a generalization. However, for the purposes of this paper references to the elites and land owners as a group is based on the statistics cited by Seeman and Salisbury, and the extensive research of Dr. Benedict Kerkvliet.

27. Taruc, *Born of the People*, 78. See also, Kerkvliet, 68.

28. Hunt, Norling, 147.

29. Taruc, *Born of the People*, 221. See also, Kerkvliet, 148-149.

30. Kerkvliet, 116-118.

31. Kerkvliet, 71-72, 150-155.

32. Hunt, Norling, 69-70.

33. Hunt, Norling,103.

34. Kerkvliet, 103-104. MacArthur's headquarters directed the USAFFE guerrilla units they were in contact with to primarily maintain a low profile and focus on intelligence collection.

35. General Headquarters, Far East Command, *Brief History of the G-2 Section, GHQ, SWPA and Affiliated Units* (Tokyo: Government Printing Office, 1948), 46, Combined Arms Research Library, Fort Leavenworth, KS.

36. Manchester, 375.

37. According to Lieutenant Colonel Jesus A. Villamor, a Filipino pilot awarded the US Distinguished Service Cross and sent to the occupied Philippines by General MacArthur to coordinate with the guerrillas, Whitney was incensed by guerrilla actions that damaged infrastructure critical to the rehabilitation of the most profitable pre-war Philippine industries, particularly the sugar and lumber industries, even if that infrastructure was materially aiding the Japanese war effort (Seeman, Salisbury, 39-40).

38. Manchester, 377.

39. *Brief History of the G-2 Section*, 32.

40. Assistance Chief of Staff, G-2, Army Forces Western Pacific, *Philippine Islands Rehabilitation, Intelligence Assessment No. 29* (Lansdale Papers, Box 74, Hoover Institution Archives, Stanford University, Palo Alto, CA), 4.

41. Memorandum by the Secretary of State to President Truman, 18 April 1946. *Foreign Relations of the United States, 1946*, 3 (Washington, DC: Government Printing Office, 1971), 874.

42. The United States High Commissioner in the Philippines (McNutt) to Mr. Richard R. Ely, of the Office of United States High Commissioner, Washington, 18 January 1946, *Foreign Relations of the United States, 1946*, 3, 865.

43. Manchester, 375.

44. Manchester, 377. According to Karnow, MacArthur helped Roxas' overcome his collaborationist past by "summarily exhonerat[ing]" him after he was captured by US forces. When MacArthur reunited with Roxas he publicly embraced him and reinstated him in the Philippine Army as a brigadier general, and claimed that Roxas had been a member of the underground, providing vital intelligence to MacArthur's headquarters, though a later investigation was never able to prove the claim. MacArthur next directed President Osmeña to convene the legislature. Since most of the congressmen had collaborated with the Japanese, and because Roxas represented the senior collaborator in congress, it was almost assured he would be voted senate president, giving him control of the upper house, and making him chairman of the Appointments Committee. This committee was responsible for approving all governmental appointments, giving him significant leverage over the president, and significant power to dispense patronage to supporters or coerce potential opponents (Karnow, 627-628).

45. Manchester, 416-417.

46. Kerkvliet, 199-200; See also Karnow, 628. In August 1945, MacArthur ordered the release of 5,000 collaborators, many of them from the political and elite establishment.

47. Hunt, Norling, 71.

48. Taruc, *Born of the People*, 190.

49. Taruc, *Born of the People*, 191. According to Taruc's claim, at least 109, but as many as 160, men of Huk Squadron 77 were massacred by Colonel Adonais Carlos Maclang's forces in Malolos on 7 February 1945. See also Kerkvliet, 115, and Karnow, 650.

50. Taruc, 196, 198.

51. The connection between the Huks and external communist support remains a point of contention. According to the Huk military commander, Luis Taruc, at the beginning of the war they only had two books to reference in developing their organization–Edgar Snow's Red Star Over China, and a translated copy of Chu The's book on guerrilla tactics (Taruc, *Born of the People*, 63). A military intelligence assessment of guerrilla organizations in Luzon prior to the invasion in late 1944 noted that the Huk movement "was said to be modeled [on] Chinese communist organizations, and it was probable that Chinese had a hand in the early organization" (Ward, 9). The only recorded Communist Chinese material contribution to the Huks was the Wa Chi, or Squadron 48, which wasn't formed until May of 1942. This squadron was drawn not from Chinese smuggled in from mainland China, but rather from the Chinese community of Manila. Amongst that community were veterans of Mao's 8th Route Army, who became the backbone of the squadron. Due to battlefield successes, the organization and methods of the Wa Chi were widely copied by other Huk squadrons (Taruc, *Born of the People*, 75-76). Finally, in light of the difficulties facing Mao's forces in China it is unlikely that the Huks were receiving any real aid or support from China during the war.

52. Clarence A. Boonstra interview.

53. Karnow, 638.

54. Kerkvliet, 148.

55. Kerkvliet, 152. Following World War II the Philippine Constabulary was renamed the Military Police Command. It would revert to the name Philippine Constabulary by 1948.

56. Journal of Edward Lansdale, No. 7, 4 February 1947, (Lansdale Papers, Box 72, Hoover Institution Archives, Stanford University, Palo Alto, CA). Subsequent references will omit publication information, as all of Lansdale's journal entries were found in the same box in his papers at the Hoover Institution Archives. See also Kerkvliet, 149.

57. Kerkvliet, 146.

58. Kerkvliet, 151.

59. Kerkvliet, 153.

60. Kerkvliet, 169. The HMB would continue to be popularly referred to as the Huks, so the terms Huk and HMB will be used interchangeably from this point forward.

61. 'Daniel Marston, *Rock in an Angry Sea: The Indian Army 1945-1947*, (Cambridge: Cambridge University Press, 2013), TBC.

62. Douglas Porch, "French Imperial Warfare 1945-62," in *Counterinsurgency in Modern Warfare* (Oxford: Osprey Publishing, 2008), 80.

63. The United States High Commissioner in the Philippines (McNutt) to Mr. Richard R. Ely, of the Office of United States High Commissioner, Washington, 18 January 1946, *Foreign Relations of the United States, 1946*, 3, 865. Ironically, the US contradicted this policy early on by supporting France's retention of Indochina after the war. Rising anti-communist sentiment overrode a recommendation from the Office of Strategic Services (OSS) that America recognize Ho Chi Minh's government because the US supported him during World War II.

64. Macdonald, 141.

65. The Secretary of War (Patterson) to the Secretary of State, Washington, 29 November 1946, *Foreign Relations of the United States, 1946*, 3, 934.

66. The United States High Commissioner in the Philippines (McNutt) to Mr. Richard R. Ely, of the Office of United States High Commissioner, Washington, 18 January 1946, 865.

67. Clarence A. Boonstra interview. See also Karnow, 693.

68. Memorandum by the Secretary of State to President Truman, 18 April 1946. *Foreign Relations of the United States, 1946*, 3, 874.

69. Macdonald, 131.

70. Journal of Edward Lansdale, No. 1, 30 October 1946.

71. Kerkvliet, 151.

72. Kerkvliet, 150.

73. Seeman, Salisbury, 53. See also Karnow, 643. This was despite the fact that several seated members of the Philippine Congress were still under enditment for treason stemming from their collaboration with the Japanese.

74. Abraham Chapman, "Note on the Philippine Elections," *Pacific Affairs* 19, no. 2 (June 1946): 198.

75. Kerkvliet, 118. See also James Putzel, *A Captive Land: The Politics of Agrarian Reform in the Philippines* (London: Catholic Institute for International Relations, 1992), 83.

76. Consolidated timeline of events from 1945-1954.

77. John F. Melby, Philippine Desk Officer, Washington, DC (1948-1953); interviewed by Charles Stuart Kennedy (June 1989), ADST/CRS.

78. Central Intelligence Agency, *The Current Situation in the Philippines*, 30 March 1949 (CIA Freedom of Information Act Library, http://www.foia.cia. gov/search .asp, accessed 27 August 2012). See also Cliff Forster, Branch Public Affairs Officer, USIS, Davao (1949-1952); interviewed by G. Lewis Schmidt (29 May 1990). See also Macdonald, 133, 139, 144.

79. Economic Survey Mission, 12.

80. Economic Survey Mission, 47.

81. Economic Survey Mission, 12. See also Leslie R. Bungaard, "Philippine Local Government," *The Journal of Politics* 19, No. 2 (May 1957): 271. These teachers were often forced to sell their anticipated paychecks to moneylenders at rates as high as forty percent interest

82. Economic Survey Mission, 90.

83. Economic Survey Mission, 95.

84. Economic Survey Mission, 17.

85. Economic Survey Mission, 24.

86. Journal of Edward Lansdale, No. 12, 30 March 1947. Luis Taruc lists 76 barrios by name in Central Luzon that were either completely or partially destroyed during this period (Taruc, *Born of the People*, 243-244).

87. Harold Isaacs, "The Danger in the Philippines, Part 2," *Manila Times*, 14 June 1950 (Myron Cowen Papers, Box 4, Truman Library, Independence, MO). See also Macdonald, 138.

88. Isaacs.

89. Mateo del Castillo, Luis Taruc, Manuel Roxas, "Taruc-Roxas Correspondence" *Far Eastern Survey* 15, No. 20 (9 October 1946): 315.

90. Joseph T. Hart, *The Huk Insurgency in the Philippines, 1946-1954*, Conflict Analysis Division, Strategic Studies Counterinsurgency Series (Bethesda, MD: Research Analysis Corporation, 1963), 8.

91. Isaacs, "The Danger in the Philippines, Part 2."

92. Kerkvliet, 247.

93. Romeo Taruc, interview with the author, Angeles City, Pampanga, 18 October 2012. See also, Memorandum of Conversation between Anastas Mikoyan and Mao Zedong, 3 February 1949, Cold War International History Project (CWIHP), www.CWIHP.org, by permission of the Woodrow Wilson International Center for Scholars. In this 1949 conversation Mao informed Soviet Minister of Foreign Trade, Anastas Mikoyan, that the Chinese Communist Party maintained contact with communist parties throughout Asia,

but that "all work of liaison with com[munist] parties is carried out through a special comrade, located in Hong Kong, but it is conducted poorly." Mikoyan then warned Mao that in "the membership of the politburo of such com[munist] parties as those of the Philippines . . . there are many American and English spies, therefore the CCP must be careful in relations with them." This poor, and limited, contact between the Chinese communists and the PKP and Huks, and suspicion on the part of the Chinese, suggests that the Philippine communists were effectively isolated from external support.

94. Headquarters, Department of the Army, *Field Manual 3-24: Counterinsurgency* (Washington, DC: Government Printing Office, 2006), 1-9, 1-16.

95. Karnow, 648

96. Macdonald, 134.

97. Edward G. Lansdale, *In the Midst of Wars: An American's Mission to Southeast Asia* (New York: Harper and Row, 1972), 29. An additional, widely repeated anecdote of the period was that "in Lanao Province, another Liberal Party stronghold, the people said that "even the trees and monkeys voted in favor of the administration" (Taruc, *He Who Rides the Tiger*, 59).

98. Harold Isaacs, "The Danger in the Philippines, Part 5," *Manila Times*, date unavailable (Myron Cowen Papers, Box 4, Truman Library, Independence, MO). See also Taruc, *He Who Rides the Tiger*, 60.

99. Harold Isaacs, "The Danger in the Philippines, Part 4," *Manila Times*, 16 June 1950 (Myron Cowen Papers, Box 4, Truman Library, Independence, MO). Mr. Alfredo Lim, a member of the Manila police force in the early 1950s confirmed that police were used as "the private armies of the mayors." At the time, the police forces were not professionalized. When a new mayor was elected, as part of the spoils of victory, he would appoint a new force. These policemen were generally loyal supporters with little to no law enforcement experience. The situation changed in October 1950 when the Philippine Civil Service first instituted standardized examinations as a requirement for police service. Alfredo Lim, interview with the author, Manila City Hall, 22 October 2012. For a short biographical sketch of Mr. Lim see Appendix C.

100. Lansdale, *In the Midst of Wars*, 69.

101. In an interview with the author, Father Jack Schumacher recounted his first interaction with the Huks. A Huk unit came to his seminary in Novaliches, Manila, and demanded food and supplies. The Jesuit priests explained that they only had enough food to feed themselves. The Huks apologized to the priests and then left. However, as they departed the Huks proceeded to take food and shoes from the Filipino construction workers employed by the seminary. In the 1960s Father Schumacher had the opportunity to meet Luis Taruc and recounted this experience. Upon hearing this, Taruc acknowledged the positive treatment afforded the priests, but then claimed the Huk unit "must have been a splinter

group" because of their treatment of the workers (John Schumacher, interview with the author, 17 October 2012, Jesuit Residence, Ateneo University, Manila).

102. Kerkvliet, 179-180.

103. The term existential threat, as used here, refers to a threat to the existence of stability in the Philippines and to the actual government. By this point in the Huk rebellion the government was facing political and economic crisis, and significant Huk military victories may have toppled the government.

104. Isaacs, "The Danger in the Philippines, Part 5."

Chapter 3
New Beginnings

The weakness in our position here is that we no longer have authority. This leaves us only influence, of which we must make best possible use.

> — Ambassador Myron Cowen, The Ambassador in the Philippines (Cowen) to the Department of State, February 15, 1951.[1]

By 1949, US government officials knew the situation in the Philippines was critical. The arrival of the new decade would shed light on just how grim the situation was. The massively corrupt 1949 general elections gave the incumbent Elpidio Quirino another four years at the helm of a country without a rudder. President Quirino, while adept at playing Philippine politics, was not the type of figure the country needed to repair the social fissures and economic problems it faced. Additionally, the practice of dispensing patronage to loyalists ensured the Armed Forces of the Philippines (AFP) and PC ranks contained men more concerned with demonstrating loyalty to political masters than to upholding their constitutional oaths. Complicating matters for the US was the initiation of hostilities on the Korean peninsula and a host of other international events, distracting US attention from the Philippines, though this may have proved to be good for the situation.

The emerging Philippine crisis called for a strong leader of good moral character and integrity. Elpidio Quirino lacked integrity, and was both physically, ethically, and morally weak. In a memorandum from Secretary of State Dean Acheson's office to President Truman, Qurinio was described as stubborn, vain, arrogant, petty, vindictive, micro-managing, egotistical, politically and morally irresponsible, and that "all indications are that he would prefer to see his country ruined than compromise with his insatiable ego or accept outside assistance on any terms except his own."[2] Quirino's own family did not help the situation. His brother, Antonio "Tony" Quirino, a judge for the People's Court, was seen as a "sinister character who seems to be mixed up in all sorts of dubious transactions in the Philippines," and would continue to play a role in Elpidio Quirino's increasingly authoritarian actions.[3]

Quirino essentially mortgaged the legitimacy of the Philippine government to ensure his own reelection. While he succeeded in holding on to the presidency, the election politically weakened him within the Liberal Party and exacerbated the security situation in the provinces.[4]

Threatening to expose his fellow party leaders' improprieties mitigated this weakness, but he was in an increasingly precarious position.[5] Indeed, by June 1950 Central Intelligence Agency (CIA) analysts were predicting Quirino's imminent downfall, noting that "despite an oppressive disregard for civil rights, [he] has been unable to maintain law and order, and has permitted excessive graft, corruption, and inefficiency."[6]

By 1950 Philippine society was increasingly fractured. The Huks were capitalizing on class divisions exacerbated by World War II and the previous four years of misgovernment. The Huks easily pointed out the links between the elites and the government, as the government was *composed* of the elite and land owning class.[7] However, class division was not the only ill plaguing Philippine society. Rival political factions also divided communities across the country.[8] As mentioned previously, following the results of the 1949 election supporters of Quirino's opponent, Jose Laurel, rose up in a short lived but violent revolt in his home province of Batangas. Unfortunately this kind of factional conflict was typical of the time, and by 1950 American officials assumed that violence would accompany future elections.[9]

If the sociopolitical problems were not enough, by 1950 the Philippine government was on the verge of bankruptcy. American aid money helped to improve the situation, but by late 1949 the US government insisted on dispatching an economic mission to the Philippines to assess the severity of the problem. In 1950 the Economic Survey Mission to the Philippines, led by former Under Secretary of the Treasury Daniel W. Bell, compiled a concise report on the problems facing the country. The results of the Bell survey mission were unsettling:

> There are officials in the Philippine Government who are aware of the dangers in this pervading economic unbalance between production and needs, between prices and wages, between Government expenditures and taxes, between foreign exchange payments and receipts. Some of them understand the reasons why these difficulties arose; but the measures that could halt the deterioration have not been put into effect. Inefficiency and even corruption in the Government service are widespread. Leaders in agriculture and in business have not been sufficiently aware of their responsibility to improve the economic position of the lower income groups. The public lacks confidence in the capacity of Government to act firmly to protect the interests of all the people. The situation is being exploited by the Communist-led Hukbalahap movement to incite lawlessness and disorder.[10]

President Truman was alarmed at the findings. The situation was so bad that before Bell even left the Philippines he informed Washington that the government would collapse unless it received an emergency loan of $20-30 million.[11] Among the governmental departments requiring immediate assistance was the Department of National Defense which was on the verge of being unable to pay its soldiers.[12]

The Armed Forces of the Philippines and the Philippine Constabulary were at a low ebb by 1950. While they were well equipped with modern weapons, provided through the Joint United States Military Advisory Group (JUSMAG), their primary problems were leadership and morale. [13] Officials in the US embassy understood the AFP needed a change in leadership, but they lacked the leverage necessary to bring about such changes.[14] Poor leadership and morale contributed to a lack of discipline within the security forces, manifested in their abuse of civilians during operations, perhaps the worst of which occurred on Good Friday, 1950. On that day, "army troops massacred 100 men, women, and children in Bacalor, Pampanga, and burned 130 homes in retaliation for the killing of one of their officers."[15] When combating the insurgency the security forces, particularly the PC, were proving counterproductive. Popular support was critical to successful prosecution of the campaign, and the "Constabulary [was] alienating the populace by their actions."[16] Militarily, if Huk successes and expanding capabilities continued and AFP defeats and professional atrophy continued, the CIA believed the Huks would be capable of toppling the government.[17]

Unfortunately, professional atrophy appeared to be the preferred course for the armed forces. Officers "often engaged in large-scale corruption," and "were often implicated in Manila-based scandals."[18] Offensive operations usually only occurred as a result of some Huk operation that "made political waves in Manila."[19] Frustrated, underpaid soldiers, garrisoned in local barrios for extended periods, with little supervision preyed on the local population, while "those above [them] seemed as equally unconcerned, more interested in graft, corruption, and a comfortable life than with fighting [the Huks]."[20] While average soldiers may have been the ones abusing the people, the crux of the problem was clearly in the officer corps.

One of the main causes of this crisis of professionalism was the politicization of the officer corps. A patronage system existed whereby politicians were able to reward family, friends, and supporters with military positions.[21] According to Carlos Romulo, the system was perpetuated by "the mutual protective society sponsored . . . by the army officers' corps."[22]

Once in position, the system continued to promote those with the best political connections over those with combat experience.[23] "Conditions were deplorable in the Department of Defense and worse in the uniformed forces. The latter especially had been weakened by the almost complete infiltration of political influence and machination. Officers openly intrigued for promotion and plush assignments."[24] Without a substantial shock to the system the situation was unlikely to change, as there was no incentive to change.

In 1950, events elsewhere in the world kept the United States actively engaged in almost all theaters. The previous year saw the Soviet Union detonate an atomic bomb, a communist victory in China, and communist regimes take power in East Germany and Hungary. Malaya, Indochina, and Burma were all in the midst of communist insurgencies and in June 1950 North Korean forces invaded South Korea, initiating a conventional war on the Korean peninsula. In light of the rapidly expanding communist threat, American decolonization policy took a back seat to preventing communist success in the Philippines.[25]

For US officials in the Philippines, the publication of NSC-68 by the National Security Council in April 1950 provided the basis for future American policy in the Philippines. Those parts of the document specifically addressing concerns in Asia properly identified the problems facing officials in the Philippines, as not simply economic but also institutional and administrative.[26] As one political scientist noted, the US moved away from a policy of bolstering, or almost blindly supporting the existing regime, and towards a policy of quid pro quo reforms.[27]

With Washington's attention focused elsewhere, US officials in the Philippines had significant leeway for local action, as long as those actions met America's policy objectives. Under a weak or indecisive ambassador this could have spelled disaster, but the embassy was ably led at the time by Ambassador Myron Cowen. When Lansdale finally joined Cowen and the rest of the US mission in the Philippines, the leeway afforded them by Washington's distraction allowed US officials in the Philippines to develop local solutions to local problems.[28]

Only a week before the publication of NSC-68, the US Counselor of Embassy Vinton Chapin, assessed the security situation in the Philippines in a dispatch to Secretary of State Acheson. Chapin believed the US military aid program and JUSMAG were "well-equipped to advise with respect to ordinary matters of military organization and operations but [they] have inadequate knowledge of and expertise with political subversion and guerrilla warfare," and that perhaps the JUSMAG mandate needed to expand beyond just an advisory role. He further noted that the equipment being supplied to the Philippines was "not well-suited to the requirements of guerrilla warfare."[29] Interestingly, Chapin noted the need for the proper US military personnel to advise on counterinsurgency, yet neglected to note that AFP personnel were inadequate to the task, focusing instead on their materiel. Chapin comes close to, but misses making the point that the US advisory effort needed to focus on professionalizing the AFP officer corps and improving esprit de corps.

Chapin went on to recommend that the Department of Defense assign a "substantial" number of officers to JUSMAG with experience in guerrilla warfare - specifically mentioning colonels David D. Barrett and Frank N. Roberts, both of whom were involved with guerrilla movements in China during World War II. Chapin's vision of an expanded role for JUSMAG included the types of actions employed by the US advisory mission during the Greek Civil War, and went so far as to suggest the US "Quietly . . . move moderate-sized Army units onto the Clark Field Air Base," an idea expanded on by the Melby-Erskine Military Assistance mission to "not less than a reinforced division."[30]

As noted by Chapin, the situation called for new personnel to assist the embassy team in the Philippines. However, the Philippines was not China, and whoever was chosen to tackle the problems in the Philippines needed to have some background or understanding of the country. The US also needed a reliable partner within the Philippine government.[31] Yet existing candidates within the government's senior leadership were assessed as lacking the necessary capabilities.[32] While the situation was dire, it also provided an opportunity for change that may not have developed otherwise, and the opportunity came in the form of Edward Lansdale and Ramon Magsaysay.[33]

Lansdale's Development

Edward Lansdale truly represents a case of the right person, in the right place, at the right time. In hindsight it would seem that every aspect of his development, aided by his personality, prepared him for his role in combating the Huks. From his experiences with the Office of Strategic Services (OSS) in the Pacific theater during the war, to his post-war assignments and professional relationships, Lansdale personality and professional development prepared him for the challenges he faced in the Philippines. However, this apparent luck or providence was grounded in something more tangible.

Throughout Lansdale's autobiography and biography, it is clear that personality played an important part in his actions in the Philippines. He possessed deep convictions about the importance of his work in fighting communism, but more importantly in promoting democracy and democratic ideals.[34] Lansdale's journal, from his early days in the Philippines, demonstrates that he genuinely cared about the plight of the lower classes, particularly those in the provinces, applying blame equally to the Huks and the PC for the peasant's suffering.[35] Lansdale's genuine nature was also noted by those who came to know him personally. In describing Lansdale, Ramon Magsaysay's son noted that "he was nice. He was not rough or tough. He [had] good rapport with ordinary people. I think that's why my father got close to him, because they were both sensitive of ordinary people . . . He was sincere. He didn't ruffle feathers. He was quiet . . . he was more observing."[36] All of these characteristics contributed to a charisma that naturally attracted people to him, and allowed him to work with individuals from diverse backgrounds.

Prior to World War II he worked as an advertising executive in California, a career path that would later prove useful. During the war he found employment in the ranks of the OSS. His work with the OSS exposed him to the usefulness of clandestine and covert operations. The OSS also broadened his horizons in terms of who might prove useful in intelligence work, as he traveled the west coast of the US speaking with a broad range of experts in various fields.[37] Working with the OSS in the Pacific Theater also provided him a geographic orientation that would remain for the vast majority of his career.

Following the war, with his unconventional OSS days behind him, Lansdale was assigned to the conventional G-2 (Intelligence) section of US Army Forces Western Pacific, based in the Philippines, from 1945-1948. In this capacity, Lansdale was responsible for collecting, analyzing and presenting information on a wide range of issues. His section not only produced intelligence on security threats, such as the Huks, they were also responsible for assessing the political and economic situation.[38] While Lansdale had a staff to aid in this process, he shied away from office based assessments and analysis, preferring instead to go out and see the situation for himself.

This desire for firsthand information started as early as late 1945, when he wanted to determine why the Huks had so much popular support. Prior to an anti-Huk PC operation Lansdale looked at maps of the intended operations area and identified likely Huk escape routes. He then drove a jeep to one of the identified routes and after encountering a Huk unit, spent time talking to them, sharing beer and cigarettes as he listened to their stories.[39] The event helped shape his understanding of the Huks as individuals. It also led him to develop his own ideas about how to come to grips with the situation in the Philippines, concluding that "the first lesson is rather basic: there is no substitute for first-hand knowledge."[40]

Lansdale's rapidly increasing appreciation of the problems in the Philippines yielded a later observation that "90% of the officers hadn't the least idea of what was going on for the Wack Wack [Country Club] is still operating, and there are lots of dependents living here now and the Army has started drawing off into its own little community."[41] Lansdale made an important observation in this remark. Despite US pre-war institutional knowledge, World War II altered the fabric of Philippine society.[42] Ambassador Cowen identified a similar problem within the diplomatic corps. Part of the problem was a need for "better training of political officers and desirability they spend less time at their desks."[43] Instead of actively getting out amongst the population, Americans in the Philippines were content to isolate themselves.

Lansdale's developing empathy for the people in the Philippines also began to encompass the rank-and-file of the Huk movement. Based on his contact and interaction with Huks during his forays into the field, combined with the personality traits described earlier, Lansdale developed an appreciation of the differences between the Huk leadership and the average Huk fighter.[44] In one instance, PC officer Napoleon Valeriano invited Lansdale to observe an operation in which they surrounded a Huk base and were preparing to attack. Lansdale declined the invitation to observe from the PC forward command post because "I have broken bread and shared cans of beer with folks on both sides of this squabble, and I couldn't square with myself if I had to sit and listen to the orders being issued to kill people I knew."[45] The Huks were no longer faceless, dogmatic communists to Lansdale, but individuals with unique and perhaps justifiable motivations for fighting the government.

Just as Lansdale was growing closer to the Filipino people, the same was not true of civil-military relations between the American military and Filipino civilians. Civil-military relations were suffering during the immediate post-war years for a number of reasons, and the decision was eventually made to place the Public Information Office under the G-2 in order to reinvigorate the office with new leadership. The office had previously been led by a full colonel. Major Lansdale was given the task of rebuilding the American military's image in the Philippines through the Public Information Office.[46] This position was to prove extremely important in Lansdale's development.

As the de facto public information officer for the Philippines Ryuku Command (PHILRYCOM), Lansdale came in close contact with the editors of almost all of the major newspapers and publications in the Philippines. One of his most important contacts, Juan "Johnny" Orendain, was both Lansdale's lawyer and his subordinate in the Intelligence Division, Armed Forces Western Pacific, G-2.[47] Orendain was well known in Manila and became President Roxas' press secretary in late 1946.[48] Unlike previous press secretaries, Orendain was invited to participate in cabinet meetings, giving him unprecedented access to the executive decision-making process in Malacañan, and indirectly providing Lansdale the same access.[49] Through Orendain and other lower level government officials, and his press contacts, Lansdale developed a substantial social network that included businessmen, industrialists, and local, provincial, and national level government officials. Combined with his provincial trips that allowed him to meet with the lower classes, Lansdale's network encompassed virtually all social classes.

An early lesson in humility and relationship building came when Lansdale's superior officer in the G-2/Public Information Office departed the Philippines. The embassy public relations officer, Julius C.C. Edelstein was departing around the same time and had performed similar functions and traveled in the same circles. Lansdale learned an important lesson from their respective legacies:

> Julius is just getting a lot of dirty cracks from the papers and he is quite annoyed. He has helped [President] Roxas with most of his speeches as well as being [Ambassador] McNutt's P.R.O., but he also goes around after a couple of drinks telling people that he has made his mark on Philippine history and is a big man in the Islands, which doesn't wash down so well with the local folks. Julius probably worked a lot harder than [Colonel] Chester but, Chester spent his time making friends. There's a moral there somewhere for Americans out in the Philippines.[50]

Even though Lansdale was quite visible in the Philippines during his service in the country, he clearly tried to take Colonel Chester's lesson in humility and relationship building to heart. When Lansdale left the Philippines with his family in 1948, more than a hundred Filipinos came to see them off.[51] He left his mark on the hearts of his Filipino friends during his first assignment, but it would take his next assignment in the Philippines for him to leave his mark on the country's history.[52]

Magsaysay's Development

Unknown to Lansdale during his first assignment in the Philippines, his future partner in the struggle against the Huks was developing along a parallel track. Congressman Ramon Magsaysay was building a name for himself not only in his home province of Zambales, but on the national scene as well. By 1950, Ramon Magsaysay had solidified his understanding of the problem and what was needed to reverse his country's slide into chaos. However, his development as a leader began long before he burst onto the stage in 1950.

Magsaysay spent his early years in Zambales as the son of a trade school teacher, in a simple house. An early life lesson impressed on Magsaysay the cost of adhering to principles and ideals. His father failed the son of the trade schools superintendent, and was fired.[53] Despite the family's crisis, Ramon Magsaysay took the lesson to heart and continued to learn from his very principled father. Magsaysay started working at the age of seven and continued to work throughout his childhood in order to help make ends meet for his family. During this period he began working in his father's small blacksmith shop where he developed a lifelong interest in all things mechanical, and which started him down a road that would lead to the presidency.[54]

Magsaysay became a mechanic for the Try Tran bus company in 1931. Working for Try Tran brought him intervals of relative prosperity and absolute misery as the fortunes of the company rose and fell. He and his newly formed family learned what it was to live in poverty.[55] Yet his association with the bus company also brought him opportunity. When the Japanese invaded the Philippines in late 1941, the company was commandeered by the US military to transport soldiers. Magsaysay volunteered his services and because of his skills was commissioned as a captain in the 31st Division's motor pool, under the command of Colonel Napoleon Valeriano.[56]

When Bataan fell, Magsaysay and his unit were still in Zambales. Rather than surrender, they organized themselves into a guerrilla unit under the command of Colonel Gyles Merrill.[57] As an officer in the Zambales Guerrillas, as they came to be known, Magsaysay excelled at motivating his fellow Filipino guerrillas, but held one belief that caused him grief with both his countrymen and the Americans. He believed in reconciliation with collaborators. Rather than executing or assassinating collaborators, Magsaysay argued on their behalf. This trait would continue beyond the war in his views of the Huks and their supporters.[58] Despite differences of opinion regarding collaboration, Magsaysay eventually rose to command the Zambales Guerrillas, developing an impressive operational record.[59] When liberation came, MacArthur asked for nominations for provincial military governors from the guerrilla leaders and Colonel Merrill submitted Magsaysay's name. Magsaysay was appointed military governor of Zambales province in February 1945, starting him on his post-war political career.[60]

Though his career as the military governor of Zambales was a short two months this post, combined with his reputation as a guerrilla leader, brought him to the attention of Manuel Roxas. Roxas invited him to Manila and offered him a seat on his ticket for the upcoming election in 1946.[61] Magsaysay turned him down, but later relented under pressure from former guerrilla comrades that he run for congress, helping establish a large popular base within the province.[62] His election campaign ironically pitted him against a man chosen by Roxas after Magsaysay's initial refusal. Despite the party machinery backing Roxas' chosen candidate, Magsaysay won by the largest majority in the history of Zambales.[63] The attributes that characterized Magsaysay the man, helped make Magsaysay the congressman.

The attributes that made Magsaysay so popular with the people derived from two main sources. The first were his humble origins and the traits imbued in him while living in Zambales. Out of those origins came his belief in hard work and uncompromising principles.[64] The people related to Magsaysay because they saw something of themselves in him, and vice versa. This built a strong bond of trust between Magsaysay and the people, and he was unwilling to break that bond of trust by taking advantage of his position for personal gain. Magsaysay's son remembered that as president, when his family would host family and friends at gatherings at Malacañan Palace, his father would deduct the cost of the event from his monthly salary.[65] Magsaysay wanted to demonstrate integrity and character by personally setting the example.

Magsaysay's leadership by example, developed during his days as a guerrilla leader, characterized his other main attribute. One of Magsaysay's lieutenants related advice given him by Magsaysay that "a leader must go through the same difficulties of his men if he is to understand them."[66] Once in office, Magsaysay translated this wartime lesson from service to his fellow guerrillas to his fellow citizens. The example Magsaysay set fostered a strong sense of loyalty not only amongst his supporters, but also in converts to his cause. Ramon Magsaysay, Jr. noted the story of Eddie

Ngolab, a former Huk that his father pardoned while Secretary of National Defense. Ngolab was allowed to join the AFP and was subsequently assigned as a bodyguard to the Magsaysay family, specifically Ramon, Jr. The former Huk remained with the family throughout the presidency. Following President Magsaysay's untimely death, Ngolab requested to remain with the now former-first family, and did so until Ramon, Jr. completed college.[67]

Coming from the provinces and humble origins, Magsaysay had an almost innate sociocultural understanding. This in turn fostered his empathy for the average Filipino, with whom he readily identified. These qualities gave Magsaysay a powerful popular base that would serve him well in the years to come, but that did not necessarily translate into the type of support or recognition necessary to on the national stage. As 1949 drew to a close there was no indication that in less than a year Magsaysay would be the Secretary of National Defense. In fact, given the volatile nature of Philippine politics and rigidity of the social classes, the Americans took a risk in backing him.

Why Magsaysay?

History should not assume that Magsaysay was the American's logical or only choice for a partner. Reuters correspondent Peter C. Richards, a contemporary and acquaintance of Magsaysay and Lansdale, believed that Lansdale could have had the same success in promoting his houseboy, such were Lansdale's skills.[68] Lansdale's extensive contacts from his early days in the Philippines exposed him to many, if not most, of the most important political, business, and social leaders in the country. So why did the United States choose to back Magsaysay?

Magsaysay was not from the political establishment in the Philippines. While this made him popular with the lower and middle classes, he faced formidable opposition from the entrenched ruling class. Philippine politics was characterized by what has been termed dynasticism or the rule of powerful political families or patronage networks. While "factionalism and patron-client ties have been isolated as the main structures of Philippine politics," Dr. Mina Roces argues that these are symptoms of the larger, underlying problem of "*politica de familia*" or kinship politics.[69] The families that maintained traditional control over the provinces had significant support bases stemming from the old practice of *caciquism*, or political control through local political bosses.[70] Traditionally, political success rested on the degree of support derived from these families.

In addition to Magsaysay's lack of political pedigree, he also lacked the refinement normally associated with service at the national executive level. In a letter from Carlos Romulo, Philippine ambassador to the US, to Ambassador Myron Cowen, Romulo discussed a press conference held for Magsaysay in Washington, DC. In response to press questions during the event, Magsaysay "unfortunately tried to answer and did not know who Adenauer and Schumacher are, did not know what the Bonn Treaty is, nor the difference between Teheran and Yalta."[71] In light of Lansdale's exposure to a broad cross-section of Philippine leadership, it would seem he could have chosen someone more refined and from the existing political establishment. Lansdale once described his friend, experienced Filipino politician Lorenzo Tañada as "the defender of almost forgotten national ethics," a good starting qualification by any standard.[72] Ambassador Carlos Romulo represented another option. He was well known to the Americans, having come ashore with MacArthur at Leyte in 1945, and then serving as the Philippine ambassador to the United States.[73] Both Tañada and Romulo were polished and experienced politicians. Despite other options, Lansdale and the Americans must have been looking at other qualities.

Magsaysay's personality played a role, and personality was extremely important if the US was going to overcome the power of the entrenched ruling class. His popularity with the people gave him mass appeal that would help to shield him from inevitable attacks by opponents within the ruling class. Frisco San Juan, a former Magsaysay lieutenant, shed light on the American decision to choose Magsaysay over someone closer to the ruling class. "We are hero worshipers. I would say, between a man who you would love and worship as your leader, and an institution, like say, democracy . . . what's democracy all about? I love this man! That's how I think [we] behave."[74] By 1950, the Philippines needed a hero, not a representative of the old order.

The US took a gamble by backing a man who was capable of developing such a large, popular base of support. Compounding the American gamble was that they were sponsoring Magsaysay against the vested interests of the existing establishment. Instead of serving as a rallying point or unifying force for the whole country, there was a risk that Magsaysay might divide the classes further. During a local political race in Negros Province, opposition candidate Moises Padilla was murdered at the behest of the provincial governor Rafael Lacson. Padilla's body was hung in the street as a warning against challenging the existing order. Upon hearing of the case, Magsaysay immediately went to the town, retrieved the body of Padilla and personally carried it through the streets, and subsequently arrested Lacson. The much publicized event incensed President Quirino, as Lacson was "one of Quirino's biggest vote manufacturers."[75]

Lacson was from the establishment, and Magsaysay's actions directly threatened that establishment. Even more damaging, in the eyes of the elites, was the popular outpouring of support from the lower classes that prevented Magsaysay experiencing any real repercussions for his actions.[76] Widespread popular support of the masses could be dangerous if Magsaysay was not committed to democratic ideals. In the end, trust was arguably one of the most important factors in the US selection of Magsaysay as its partner. Lansdale and the US had to trust that once in power, Magsaysay would not consolidate power in an authoritarian regime, relying on popular support.

With the decision made in favor of Magsaysay in the spring of 1950, a delegation of American officials traveled to Manila to work for his appointment as Secretary of National Defense.[77] The delegation arrived none too soon, as a political dispute between Quirino and Speaker of the House Eugenio Perez threatened to rip the government apart. Perez was threatening Quirino's impeachment if he did not step down. In turn Quirino was likely to fire the Secretary of National Defense and assume the position himself in order to forestall the impeachment.[78] Such an act would have at best undermined US foreign policy in the Far East, and at worst, doomed democracy in the Philippines. Making matters worse, the Huks launched major, coordinated offensives in a number of provinces in Luzon, highlighting the Philippine government's weakness.[79]

Developing the Team

President Elpidio Quirino appointed Ramon Magsaysay as Secretary of National Defense on 31 August 1950, and Magsaysay assumed his duties the next day. Within a week of Magsaysay's appointment, Edward Lansdale was once again in the Philippines. Lansdale and Magsaysay appear to have seen eye to eye on many of the actions necessary to avert the growing crisis in the Philippines when they were discussing the situation from the safety of Washington.[80] They were now responsible for putting those ideas into action.

Lansdale's guidance from Washington was sufficiently broad to provide him leeway to execute his mission as necessary, but it also had a clear intent to guide his actions. His mission was to:

> Protect American interests in the Philippines and to consolidate
> a power base for Ramon Magsaysay . . . provide counsel and
> support to the new secretary of national defense, influence the

revitalization of the Philippine Army, help the government make progress in its war against the Huks, urge political reform upon the government, and . . . help Filipinos have an honest election in the November 1951 balloting.[81]

While the tasks were daunting, Washington's intent was much simpler. The Office of Policy Coordination (OPC) wanted Lansdale to help the Philippine government defeat the Huks in any way he could, and "it was up to me to figure out how best to do this."[82] As noted previously, Washington's preoccupation with events elsewhere in the world distracted official attention on the Philippines, contributing to Lansdale's freedom of action there.

In order to accomplish his assigned tasks, Lansdale arrived as a nominal member of JUSMAG, ostensibly assigned as the intelligence advisor to President Quirino. In fact, his authorities far exceeded his low rank and position. Embassy officials were supposed to cooperate with Lansdale almost without question, up to and including the ambassador and the JUSMAG chief.[83] Despite Lansdale's significant power, the memories of Lansdale's colleagues at the embassy and in JUSMAG suggest that rather than abusing or flaunting his power, he preferred instead to build consensus and support for his operations.[84] It would seem he remembered the lesson of Colonel Chester and Julius Edelstein from his previous Philippines assignment.

The first order of business had to be security sector reform. Lansdale and Magsaysay had to stabilize the deteriorating security situation before they could move forward on more ambitious projects. Some reforms were already underway. The unwieldy Philippine infantry divisions, organized and equipped on the US model, were ill suited to fighting the Huks. The result was the Battalion Combat Team (BCT) concept. The BCT organizational reform created smaller, lighter, more mobile, and more lethal, multifunctional units of 1,000-1,500 soldiers that would theoretically be more capable of engaging the Huks on their own territory.[85] Unfortunately, while the BCT reform was a major step in the right direction it was largely cosmetic. The real problem facing the AFP, even with the new BCTs, was that the same men were still leading both the Army and Constabulary.

If the peasants of Central Luzon were suffering from absentee landlordism, then the soldiers of the AFP and PC were suffering from absentee leadership. There were professional, dedicated officers within both organizations, but the officer corps was increasingly politicized, and to achieve significant rank or position, an officer needed a political patron. Officers with little or no field experience were being promoted over officers who were actively engaged in fighting the Huks in the field.[86] Essentially, the soldiers in the field felt they were fighting the war alone while their leaders were out of harm's way. Morale was at an all-time low, and the "armed forces . . . needed rehabilitation almost as much as did the country itself."[87]

As noted previously, the embassy and JUSMAG knew the AFP and PC needed new leadership, but they could only advise and apply pressure through aid. Now, with Magsaysay as Secretary of National Defense they had an ally in position to affect change. However, because of the politicized officer corps, it was unlikely that Magsaysay would be able to bring about any real change.[88] He needed broad authority from President Quirino to make personnel decisions if he was going to make the necessary reforms within the security forces, without them he would be impotent. This authority represented a significant increase in the power of the Secretary of National Defense, and a simultaneous diminishing of Quirino's power. Actually getting Qurinio to give Magsaysay that power would require external pressure.

The Americans were able to pressure Quirino into giving Magsaysay more power, and his new powers were not insignificant. As a result, Magsaysay had the power to promote, demote, and fire officers on the spot. [89] This one act was arguably the catalyst needed to rebuild the AFP. With his new found power, Magsaysay embarked on his soon to be famous inspection tours, literally dropping in on unsuspecting AFP units in the field. Not only was Magsaysay able to rid the field army of underperforming officers, he was able to promote good ones immediately.[90] Magsaysay established the Special Board of Inquiry to investigate abuses and improprieties within the AFP; all told Board investigations led to the removal or retirement of 400 officers.[91] The power also allowed him to reform the promotion boards. Where previously, rear echelon and staff officers with connections received the promotions, Magsaysay insisted that field officers with good combat records take priority.[92] The soldiers in the field now felt they had a champion in Manila. Morale steadily improved in the AFP, as did combat performance.

Another basic, but important initiative was increasing the pay of Filipino soldiers. Previously, AFP personnel only received 30 centavos a day. Magsaysay increased it to one peso a day, funded by US military aid. This seemingly simple move had important implications for the counterinsurgency campaign. Magsaysay knew that his soldiers had been stealing food and other basic necessities from the populace, alienating the

AFP from the people. The more than threefold increase in pay allowed soldiers to pay for supplies.[93] During Magsaysay's inspection tours he was also checking on his soldier's welfare, as "the underdog of the army was certainly the common soldier who was battling the Huks in the field."[94] The new Secretary endeavored to improve the average soldier's lot in life and as a result *esprit de corps* gradually returned to the armed forces.[95]

Even with improving morale and combat performance, the AFP faced a stiff fight. By early 1950 estimates put Huk strength at around fifteen thousand armed fighters, with an active support base of around one million.[96] During Lansdale's first weeks in the Philippines he reinitiated contact with local friends from his first tour in the country. He wanted to understand why the Huks were succeeding and government failing. The picture his friends painted was not good, and most of it stemmed from government and security force abuses of power. It appeared as though Quirino's administration was assuming the trappings of an authoritarian regime.[97]

Reminiscent of his first tour in the Philippines, Lansdale wanted to get outside of the protective bubble of Manila that few embassy or JUSMAG officials ventured beyond. JUSMAG policy for members of the US government in the Philippines severely restricted travel throughout many parts of the country. While this security measure improved the safety of US personnel, it also blinded the embassy. Without the ability to travel freely, the embassy was forced to rely largely on the word of their personal and professional contacts. Not surprisingly, most of those contacts were from the elite and land owning class. Using the authority given him by OPC, Lansdale requested that Major General Leland Hobbs waive the policy for his team in the Philippines.[98] With uninhibited freedom of movement, Lansdale quickly returned to his old habit of getting out into the countryside.

Lansdale's contact with his old friends, and more importantly with civilians in the provinces, gave him pause. While some of the Huks actions may have been reprehensible, they appeared justifiable to the peasants of Central Luzon given the Philippine government's repressive actions.[99] Between the corrupt government and abusive security forces, more and more people were either actively or passively supporting the Huk movement. The people felt they no longer had a stake in the survival of the government. Before they could reverse Huk successes, Lansdale and Magsaysay had to find a way to rebuild the relationship between citizen and government.

The Team in Action

Magsaysay achieved an important victory early in his tenure as Secretary of National Defense. A mid-level Huk leader, Tarciano Rizal, approached Magsaysay under the guise of seeking amnesty and reconciliation with the government. His real mission was to assassinate the new secretary. However, Rizal apparently had a change of heart because of a long conversation he had with Magsaysay. Rather than just reconciling with the government, Rizal provided Magsaysay information on how to locate the PKP Politburo.[100] On 18 October 1950 the AFP launched raids across Manila, netting more than a hundred PKP members, a number of Politburo members, and literally tons of documents. As useful as the event was in terms of intelligence, AFP morale, and positive publicity, it did not solve the immediate problem facing Magsaysay and Lansdale.

They had to identify ways to regain popular support and trust in the AFP. It was not simply a question of increasing military effectiveness against the Huks. Magsaysay's internal reforms were gaining traction, but it was an uphill battle against an entrenched establishment, that would take time. They needed to develop programs that would begin siphoning away the Huk support base, improve the AFP image, and alleviate the conditions of the Filipino people. Unfortunately, the Roxas and Quirino administrations had made promises before with little follow through. Whatever programs Magsaysay and Lansdale developed had to be derived from empathy for the plight of the people, and based on an understanding of the sociocultural condition of those people. Any disingenuous efforts would be viewed as simply more of the same from a government that was only concerned with self-preservation.

It would not be easy. The AFP Chief of Staff, Major General Mariano Castaneda, was a Quirino loyalist and hindered the development of Magsaysay's initiatives. From Castaneda's point of view, Magsaysay was simply a "guerrilla major," with no real military experience or background.[101] Additionally, Magsaysay could only affect half the problem, as the Secretary of the Interior administered the Constabulary, while provincial governors maintained operational control of the PC units in their provinces.[102] Magsaysay was able to bring the PC under his authority on 23 December 1950, causing a significant uproar within the entrenched establishment.[103] The PC had been the establishment's tool of choice in targeting the peasant movement, as the governors generally came from the landowning establishment. Magsaysay's control of the PC stripped the establishment of a significant degree of power.

While the establishment no longer controlled the PC as they once did, they still had the paramilitary Civilian Guards. According to Charles T. R. Bohannon and Colonel Napoleon Valeriano, both of whom played important roles in the Huk campaign, Magsaysay attempted to disband the Civilian Guards entirely. This proved infeasible because the AFP lacked the personnel to replace them in the provinces. The order to disband was rescinded and Magsaysay and the AFP embarked on a campaign to professionalize the Civilian Guards by sending AFP personnel "to train and control" them.[104] The program must have been successful, as former Huks credited Magsaysay with getting rid of the Civilian Guards entirely.[105]

With JUSMAG backing, Magsaysay was finally able to shake-up the combined AFP-PC leadership, though it was not quite the victory Magsaysay, Lansdale and JUSMAG hoped for. The AFP and PC chiefs of staff were both fired, but another Quirino loyalist was appointed as chief of staff, Castaneda retained his title without the authority, and Brigadier General Ramos, the former PC chief of staff, was made the director of the National Bureau of Investigation.[106] The Philippine Ambassador to the US, Joaquin M. Elizalde described Brigadier General Florencio Selga, the new Constabulary chief of staff, as a "complete Ramos stooge."[107] Despite Quirino's actions, Magsaysay pushed ahead with his plans.

Magsaysay started in the right direction to rebuild the AFPs integrity. Now he needed initiatives to tie the people back to the AFP. Even with his sociocultural understanding, Magsaysay relied on a wide range of inputs. He utilized his former guerrilla contacts in the provinces to inform him of Huk activities and initiatives, providing him with context in which to develop his own initiatives.[108] Lansdale also played an instrumental role in helping Magsaysay refine and develop his ideas further, in a unique way. Informal discussion groups developed at Lansdale's residence on Camp Murphy, where Magsaysay likewise resided.[109] These groups grew to include AFP officers from combat units, staff officers, businessmen, trusted politicians, and essentially anyone Lansdale and Magsaysay thought might have innovative and useful ideas.[110]

Easily the most memorable and oft cited Magsaysay-Lansdale initiative was the Economic Development Corps (EDCOR).[111] While this was an important initiative in terms of positive publicity, there were others of equal significance in rebuilding the bonds between the people and the AFP. When poor farmers were taken to court by wealthy landowners they generally did so alone, while the landowner was represented by lawyers. Inevitably the farmer lost. One of Magsaysay's initiatives was using AFP Judge Advocate lawyers in civilian clothes to represent farmers in court pro bono.[112] Magsaysay believed that "he who has less in life should have more in law."[113] Where they had previously had little in life and the law, Magsaysay was using the AFP to alter the equation.

Another initiative, and one that would continue into Magsaysay's presidency, was the "10 centavo telegram." Magsaysay wanted feedback from the people about AFP performance, similar to that which he got from his surprise inspection tours. In order to get this feedback he established a method for anyone to send him a telegram at an inexpensive rate, with the promise of rapid follow up. While skepticism ran deep at first, it did not take long for word to get around that the new Secretary of National Defense of was true to his word. Not only did the volume of telegrams increase exponentially, people began sending information on Huk activities in addition to reports on AFP performance.[114] These were just two of the initiatives that had a significant effect on civil-military relations in Magsaysay's first year as Secretary of National Defense.

With popular trust and confidence in the AFP on the rise, the military campaign gained traction against the Huks. However, this did not necessarily translate into trust and confidence in the Philippine government. One of the same characteristics making Magsaysay popular also limited the effectiveness of their campaign. Magsaysay was not from the traditional political establishment and might prove to be an anomaly. The bottom line was that the same men were still in power in Manila, and the November 1951 mid-term congressional and gubernatorial elections might undermine any success the AFP might have militarily.[115]

American influence was strong in the Philippines, but no matter how much Washington lobbied for clean elections, US embassy officials believed that "the elections will be honest only if Quirino sincerely wishes them to be."[116] In this case, honest elections were not in the best interest of Quirino or the Liberal Party. Despite the significant leeway Lansdale had in accomplishing his mission in the Philippines, he had to be particularly careful in handling the 1951 election. Rather than attempting to engineer the election outcome, like Liberal Party officials were planning to do, Lansdale and Magsaysay needed to ensure clean elections.[117]

Understanding Philippine society, culture, and politics, Lansdale determined their best recourse was to use the Philippine electoral code and existing laws to their advantage.[118] Partnering with the Philippine Electoral Commission, Magsaysay and the AFP provided much needed manpower to the woefully understrength government body.[119] Members of Lansdale's OPC team helped establish the National Movement for Free

Elections (NAMFREL), a non-governmental body dedicated to supporting clean elections through educating the electorate.[120] NAMFREL was ably assisted throughout the election period by Gabriel Kaplan, a progressive New York Republican with extensive experience in combatting electoral fraud and corruption in the United States.[121] Throughout the campaign season traditional intimidation methods employed by the entrenched political elite were thwarted by the AFP. Campaign rallies and speeches were guarded by AFP soldiers, permitting citizens to hear candidates from both parties equally.

Lansdale and his team stepped up their efforts on election day in November. The AFP actively patrolled the areas surrounding the polling sites and ROTC cadets served as election-watchers under Electoral Commission supervision.[122] Lansdale also orchestrated a large national and international media turnout at polling sites to cover the election, further preventing fraud. In each provincial capital, where the votes were tallied, Philippine News Service correspondents reported unofficial tallies over the radio, preventing vote tampering after the polls closed.[123]

Lansdale and Magsaysay relied on existing Philippine laws and institutions to provide the framework for clean elections.[124] They supplemented this by simply ensuring citizens understood the electoral process and had the opportunity to vote. The result was an overwhelming success for the opposition party, renewed confidence in democratic processes, increased government legitimacy, and a solid relationship between the AFP and the people. While the people felt they now had a stake in their own government, Magsaysay's AFP was seen as having provided them the opportunity to exercise their rights. The Huk high water mark came and went with the 1951 election, but the Philippines was not out of danger yet.

The success of the 1951 election was almost a Pyrrhic victory for Magsaysay's career as Secretary of National Defense. "Magsaysay was a Liberal Party defense secretary, but he saw to it that the elections would be as fair as possible. The majority of the opposition won, and of course Quirino, a Liberal, thought my father was part of that."[125] The press did not help his relationship with Quirino either, giving Magsaysay credit for the clean elections and ignoring Quirino.[126] Magsaysay was rapidly moving from an inconvenience for Quirino to a potential rival.

In little more than a year, Magsaysay and Lansdale achieved significant success in establishing the initiatives that formed the bottom-up effort to the Huk campaign. In the absence of the landlords, who once served a paternalistic function in Philippine agrarian society, Magsaysay was rapidly filling the void through his leadership of the AFP, reversing a trend that saw the Huks assuming the mantle of leadership in Central Luzon. As noted by Magsaysay subordinate Jose Crisol, the military reforms "emphasized professionalism and in-service training."[127] His leadership of the AFP and PC and programs to professionalize both organizations gained traction and were visible in the improved civil-military relationship. Magsaysay's efforts to reform the military were based on his belief that the military and the people must be inextricably linked, because "when the people are with the Army – here or any place – the Communists are finished."[128]

Magsaysay and Lansdale also succeeded in empowering the electorate, something the lower classes were denied following independence in 1946. The two men were able to achieve this, despite an entrenched and experienced political elite, because of their understanding of that elite and what it would take to counter them. The first year of Magsaysay and Lansdale's partnership also saw significant unity of effort within the US mission in the Philippines, largely because of Lansdale's ability to build consensus rather than compel support. This unity of effort led to the embassies concerted efforts to successfully protect Magsaysay from the entrenched establishment. In return, Magsaysay lived up to American faith in his abilities by garnering significant popular support and loyalty. The successes of this first year proved crucial to preventing the political crisis that would develop over the next two years from plunging the country into chaos.

Notes

1.   The Ambassador in the Philippines (Cowen) to the Department of State, February 15, 1951. *Foreign Relations of the United States, 1951*, 6, Part 2 (Washington, DC: Government Printing Office, 1977), 1507.

2.   Draft Memorandum by the Secretary of State to the President, 20 April 1950, *Foreign Relations of the United States, 1950*, 5 (Washington, DC: Government Printing Office, 1976), 1442.

3.   Memorandum by the Director of the Office of Philippine and Southeast Asian Affairs (Lacy) to the Assistant Secretary of State for Far Eastern Affairs (Rusk), 30 March 1950, *Foreign Relations of the United States, 1950*, 5, 1430. By this point, Quirino was acknowledged within the US diplomatic community as using the armed forces for his political benefit, violating constitutional and civil rights. During the 1949 elections Quirino replaced or removed non-compliant PC commanders with those willing to do his bidding, he had threatened to declare martial law if certain legislation was not passed by congress, and was considering taking on the portfolio of Secretary of National Defense shortly before being pressured into appointing Magsaysay to the post. The reference to Antonio Quirino's association with the People's Court is significant because this was the judicial body established to try collaborators after World War II. The likely gave Antonio Quirino very dubious grounds on which to collect "evidence" about former collaborators, who just happened to comprise a significant number of senior officials in all branches of government and the military.

4.   Draft Memorandum by the Secretary of State to the President, 20 April 1950, 1441.

5.   Macdonald, 138. Antonio Quirino was alleged to have had dossiers on numerous public officials with evidence implicating them in a range of improprieties that would have engulfed them in scandal.

6.   Central Intelligence Agency, *Intelligence Memorandum No. 296: Current Situation in the Philippines*, 6 June 1950 (CIA Freedom of Information Act Library, http://www.foia.cia.gov/search.asp, accessed on 27 August 2012), 1-2.

7.   Central Intelligence Agency, 3, 9.

8.   Carl H. Lande, "Parties and Politics in the Philippines," *Asian Survey* 8, No. 9 (September 1968): 728. Philippine politics of the time was characterized by frequently shifting political alliances. Rather than characteristically American party loyalty based on platforms, Filipino politicians were known to move from party to party based on individual loyalty to a patron. Individual politicians were supported by local political bosses and family leaders who delivered the votes in their local areas on election day. Rival political factions often engaged in violence and intimidation in the provinces during political campaigns, pitting villages against villages or neighborhoods against neighborhoods.

9. Central Intelligence Agency, *Memorandum to Director of Central Intelligence: Violence during Philippine Elections*, 14 October 1949 (CIA Freedom of Information Act Library, http://www.foia.cia.gov/search.asp, accessed on 27 August 2012) 1-2.

10. Economic Survey Mission, 3.

11. Macdonald, 146-147.

12. The Ambassador in the Philippines (Cowen) to the Assistant Secretary of State for Far Eastern Affairs (Rusk), 1 June 1950, *Foreign Relations of the United States, 1950*, 6, 1454.

13. *Intelligence Memorandum No. 296*, 5. In the summer of 1950 the CIA characterized the armed forces as lacking coordination between the Army and PC, failure to relieve units after long operational periods, low quality unit leadership, lack of aggressiveness in all ranks, difficult terrain, and local sympathy for the Huks.

14. The Chargé in the Philippines (Chapin) to the Secretary of State, 7 April 1950, *Foreign Relations of the United States, 1950*, 6, 1436.

15. Lawrence M. Greenberg, Analysis Branch, US Army Center of Military History, *The Hukbalahap Insurrection: A Case Study of a Successful Anti-Insurgency Operation in the Philippines, 1946-1955* (Washington, DC: Government Printing Office, 1995), 76.

16. The Chargé in the Philippines (Chapin) to the Secretary of State, 7 April 1950, 1436.

17. *Intelligence Memorandum No. 296*, 1.

18. Greenberg, 74.

19. Greenberg, 73.

20. Greenberg, 78.

21. Greenberg, 84.

22. Romulo, Gray, 129.

23. Macdonald, 143.

24. Carlos P. Romulo, *Crusade in Asia* (New York: The John Day Company, 1995), 124.

25. Draft Memorandum by the Secretary of State to the President, 20 April 1950, 1443; See also "A Report to the National Security Council by the Executive Secretary on United States Objectives and Programs for National Security" (NSC-68), 15 April 1950 (Washington, DC: Government Printing Office, 1950), 8. From here on this document will be cited as NSC-68.

26. NSC-68, 31.

27. Macdonald, 135.

28. Lawrence F. Finkelstein, "US at Impasse in Southeast Asia," *Far Eastern Survey* 19, No. 16 (27 September 1950): 168.

29. The Chargé in the Philippines (Chapin) to the Secretary of State, 7 April 1950, 1436.

30. Chapin, 1437. See also in the same volume, The Ambassador in the Philippines (Cowen) to the Secretary of State, 29 September 1950, 1495. Colonel Barrett was a US Army officer with significant experience in China, working with the Chinese Communists as part of the US Army Observation Group during WWII. Colonel Roberts was the Assistant Chief of Staff of the China-Burma-India Theater during WWII, was the US Military Attaché in Moscow from 1945-1946, and from 1950-1953 served on the National Security Council Senior Staff (Planning Board) as well as serving as the military advisor to W. Averell Harriman, Special Assistant to the President and Director for Mutual Security.

31. Draft Memorandum by the Secretary of State to the President, 20 April 1950, 1442.

32. Central Intelligence Agency, *Prospects for Stability in the Philippines*, 10 August 1950 (CIA Freedom of Information Act Library, http://www.foia.cia.gov/search.asp, accessed on 27 August 2012), 3.

33. For a condensed biographical timelines for Edward Lansdale and Ramon Magsaysay see Appendix B.

34. Lansdale, *In the Midst of Wars*, ix, 105-106; Lansdale professed the belief that the United States should not simply be anti-communist, but they must put forth a positive program that built optimism and hope. See also Lansdale, "Reunion of Nieman Fellows," lecture, Harvard University, 19 June 1957 (Lansdale Papers, Box 80, Hoover Institution Archives, Stanford University, Palo Alto, CA).

35. Journal of Edward Lansdale, No. 7, 4 February 1947.

36. Ramon Magsaysay, Jr., interview with the author, Pasay City, Manila, 22 October 2012. For a short biographical sketch of Mr. Magsaysay see Appendix C.

37. Currey, 23.

38. Headquarters, PHILRYCOM (Philippines Ryukus Command), *Weekly Activities Report*, 9 January 1948 (Lansdale Papers, Box 33, Hoover Institution Archives, Stanford University, Palo Alto, CA), 4. In the same box in Lansdale's papers are PHILRYCOM Weekly Activities Reports for the weeks of 14 November and 12 December 1947, and 9 January, 27 March, and 2 April 1948.

39. Currey, 38-39.

40. Edward Lansdale, "Lessons Learned, The Philippines: 1946-1953," Interdepartmental Course on Counterinsurgency, Foreign Service Institute,

26 September 1962, (Lansdale Papers, Box 79, Hoover Institution Archives, Stanford University, Palo Alto, CA).

41. Journal of Edward Lansdale, No. 1, 20 October 1946.

42. Karnow, 637.

43. Typed notes for a presentation on the present situation in the Philippines, 5 June 1951 (Myron Cowen Papers, Box 7, Truman Library, Independence, MO). In the same document, Cowen also identifies the following issues: "A) Need for intelligence coordination, both on a country and an area basis. B) Adequate briefing for ambassadors before going to a new post. C) Language training, even if it is only a smattering of a difficult language. D) Desirability ambassadors should familiarize themselves with all countries within their area by periodically visiting such countries. This is perhaps more valuable than regional meetings. E) Better economic staffs. [point F is quoted above]. G) More adequate coordination of activities of various agencies and better staff integration. H) Reduction of administrative overhead." These notes were likely for a meeting Ambassador Cowen had with State Department officials on 8 June 1951. In this meeting, Cowen elaborated on the points cited above. He believed that if he had had a better economic staff there would not have been a need for the Bell Economic Survey Mission. He also believed that the State Department "should not send people to the Far East who are not interested in going there. These officers . . . reflect their unhappiness, and this affects our relations with the country." In response to this, one of the officials at the meeting noted that "no one wants to be assigned to the [Far East] . . . which places those posts under a severe handicap" (Memorandum of the Under Secretary's Meeting, Prepared in the Department of State, 8 June 1951, *Foreign Relations of the United States, 1951*, 6, Part 2, 1543).

44. Journal of Edward Lansdale, No. 12, 30 March 1947.

45. Lansdale.

46. Journal of Edward Lansdale, No. 1, 20 October 1946. The US military's image in the Philippines suffered during the post-World War II years. One reason was the "bases" issue, or the US government leasing American military installations from the newly independent Philippine government for 99 years. Arguably though, the main issue was the poor behavior and indiscipline of US military personnel in the Philippines.

47. Ward, 1.

48. Journal of Edward Lansdale, No. 3, 28 November 1946.

49. Journal of Edward Lansdale, No. 5, 11 January 1947.

50. Journal of Edward Lansdale, No. 10, 5 March 1947.

51. Lansdale, *In the Midst of Wars*, 11.

52. Guillermo Sison to Edward Lansdale, personal correspondence,

18 November 1948 (Lansdale Papers, Box 33, Hoover Institution Archives, Stanford University, Palo Alto, CA). Throughout Lansdale's papers at the Hoover Institution are letters similar to the one cited here. Beyond generic letters of appreciation, the Filipino authors of these correspondences specifically noted Lansdale's personality and character, and the effect he had on the people around him.

53. Romulo, Gray, 15.

54. Romulo, Gray, 18.

55. Romulo, Gray, 42-43.

56. Romulo, Gray, 43. Napoleon Valeriano would later play an important part in not only the Huk campaign, but also in the work of Lansdale's CIA team in the Philippines, and later in Vietnam.

57. Ramon Magsaysay, Jr., interview with the author, Pasay City, Manila, 22 October 2012.

58. Romulo, Gray, 48-49.

59. Colonel (ret.) Gyles Merrill to Secretary of the Army Frank Pace, Jr., personal correspondence, 10 June 1952 (Lansdale Papers, Box 34, Hoover Institution Archives, Stanford University, Palo Alto, CA). In Colonel Merrill's letter to Secretary Pace, he recounts the Zambales Guerrilla's actions on the night of 16-17 January 1945 in response to MacArthur's orders to guerrillas in the Philippines to maximize violence against the Japanese in support of the invasion. Under Magsaysay's command, the Zambales Guerrillas destroyed 28 Japanese aircraft at San Marcelino airfield, two bridges while under enemy fire, a radio installation close to one of the invasion beaches in the vicinity of San Miguel, San Antonio, Zambales. They also blocked the Olongapo-Subic highway. The guerrillas eventually succeeded in capturing San Marcelino airfield and cleared it of hundreds of mines, thus preparing it for immediate American use. Magsaysay's operations resulted in the unopposed landing of the US XI Corps, "despite the presence of about one division of enemy troops in the Subic-Bataan area. All valid enemy resistance in the general landing area had been overcome by the Zambales Guerrilla Forces.

60. Romulo, Gray, 68.

61. Romulo, Gray, 77-78.

62. Ramon Magsaysay, Jr., interview with the author, Pasay City, Manila, 22 October 2012. Magsaysay served as an officer in the Philippine Veterans Association, and continued to nurture his contacts within the ex-guerrilla community throughout his career. The popularity of Magsaysay's former guerrilla force in Zambales province gave him uncontested support of the guerrillas, their families, and a large number of former guerrilla supporters and sympathizers. Additionally, support of the Veterans Association lent organized grass roots support during his campaign.

63. Romulo, Gray, 84.

64. Ramon Magsaysay, Jr., interview with the author, Pasay City, Manila, 22 October 2012.

65. Magsaysay.

66. Frisco San Juan, interview with the author, Quezon City, Manila, 15 October 2012. For a short biographical sketch of Mr. San Juan see Appendix C.

67. Ramon Magsaysay, Jr., interview with the author, Pasay City, Manila, 22 October 2012.

68. Currey, 89-90.

69. Roces, 184-185.

70. Putzel, 56.

71. Carlos P. Romulo to Myron Cowen, personal correspondence, 9 July 1952, (Myron Cowen Papers, Box 7, Truman Library, Independence, MO).

72. Journal of Edward Lansdale, No. 11, 19 March 1947.

73. Ramon Magsaysay, Jr., interview with the author, Pasay City, Manila, 22 October 2012.

74. Frisco San Juan, interview with the author, Quezon City, Manila, 15 October 2012.

75. Ramon Magsaysay, Jr., interview with the author, Pasay City, Manila, 22 October 2012.

76. Macdonald, 158, 162.

77. Currey, 70-72. After his initial meeting with Magsaysay, Lansdale arranged a meeting between Magsaysay and Assistant Secretary of State Livingston Merchant, then serving as liaison to the CIAs Office of Policy Coordination (OPC), General Nathan Twining, Vice Chief of Staff of the Air Force, Colonel George Chester, an intelligence community professional, Colonel Richard Stilwell, OPC Director of Far East/Plans Division, and Frank Wisner, also of OPC. Having met Magsaysay, the group decided that OPC would support Magsaysay in the Philippines. While Ambassador Cowen and JUSMAG Chief, Major General Leland Hobbs were responsible for presenting the ultimatum to President Quirino, an Office of Policy Coordination team consisting of Colonel Chester and Assistant Secretary of State Merchant traveled to the Philippines to assist and provide guidance. Other accounts of who presented the ultimatum to Quirino exist. John F. Melby of the Department of State Philippine Desk claimed in an interview that Ambassador Cowen preferred not to present the ultimatum personally as it would have soured an already tense relationship with Quirino (John F. Melby interview).

78. Macdonald, 144.

79. Macdonald, 137.

80. Currey, 70.

81. Currey, 78.

82. Lansdale, *In the Midst of Wars*, 2. As originally designed, the Central Intelligence Agency only recommended covert operations based on the intelligence it collected. A joint Department of Defense and Department of State panel then determined which operations should be carried out. The instrument created to carry out those operations was the Office of Policy Coordination (OPC). The OPC was placed under the CIA because of the intelligence collection activities provided by the Agency, but the Departments of Defense and State essentially maintained directive authority and operational control of the organization. The OPC was also funded by the CIA and its personnel were drawn from CIA ranks (Currey, 62-63).

83. Currey, 79-80.

84. Lansdale to Cowen, personal correspondence, 2 September 1960 (Myron Cowen Papers, Box 6, Truman Library, Independence, MO). Lansdale maintained positive relationships with ambassadors Myron Cowen and Raymond Spruance. Cowen and Lansdale maintained a friendship long after Cowen's departure. In a letter from Lansdale to Cowen in 1960, referring to Cowen as "Boss," Lansdale thanked Cowen for his continued interest in his career progression and promotion. Also in the letter, Lansdale felt compelled to apologize to Cowen for not inviting him to his promotion, stating that he "just kept this one in the family." Cowen also believed that Lansdale was "a better source of intelligence than all the rest of our intelligence efforts put together" (Memorandum by the Ambassador in the Philippines (Cowen) to the Secretary of State, 19 September 1951, *Foreign Relations of the United States, 1951*, 6, Part 2, 1567). As will be noted later, Ambassador Spruance played a pivotal role in securing Lansdale's return to the Philippines in early 1953 despite Department of State misgivings.

85. Fidel V. Ramos, interview with the author, Makati City, Manila, 22 October 2012. A BCT consisted of three infantry companies, a heavy weapons company with .30 and .50 caliber machine guns, 57mm and 75mm recoilless rifles, and mortars. The BCT also contained organic indirect fire support in the form of a field artillery battery of 105mm howitzers. A reconnaissance company also contained the light armored elements and trucks of the BCT. For a short biographical sketch of President Ramos see Appendix C.

86. Lansdale, *In the Midst of Wars*, 45.

87. Romulo, Gray, 126.

88. Lansdale, *In the Midst of Wars*, 25.

89. Macdonald, 145.

90. Uldarico S. Baclagon, *Lessons from the Huks Campaign in the Philippines* (Manila: M. Colcol & Company, 1960), 6.

91. Donn V. Hart, "Magsaysay: Philippine Candidate," *Far Eastern Survey* (May 1953): 67.

92. Lansdale, *In the Midst of Wars*, 45.

93. Greenberg, 85.

94. Romulo, Gray, 132.

95. Romulo, Gray, 133.

96. Lansdale, Handwritten notes for National War College Lecture, 25 March 1964 (Lansdale Papers, Box 74, Hoover Institution Archives, Stanford University, Palo Alto, CA). Despite the estimates from outside sources, during Lansdale's first embassy protocol visits and briefings upon his return to the Philippines in 1950, he recounts that the threat was significantly underrated, with some figures as low as "about a thousand" or "not more than five thousand;" his visit with Philippine intelligence impressed him as more thorough and reliable (Lansdale, In the Midst of Wars, 22).

97. Lansdale, *In the Midst of Wars*, 24-26.

98. Currey, 83. Ambassador Cowen noted the results of Hobbs' granting Lansdale's request in a telegram to the Secretary of State in March 1951. "I have impression one of reasons Hobbs has been getting better results than his predecessors is because he has been having his men go out to the provinces in order to come to direct grips with the similar problems of the Phil[ippine] mil[itary] establishment." The Ambassador in the Philippines (Cowen) to the Secretary of State, 21 March 1951, *Foreign Relations of the United States, 1951*, Part 2, 6, 1521

99. Lansdale, *In the Midst of Wars*, 24-28. Two weeks prior to his return to the Philippines, the Huks raided Camp Makabulos, a military camp approximately seventy miles north of Manila. During the raid they entered the camp's hospital and killed twenty-three military personnel and seven civilians, some of them patients still in hospital beds. The civilians in the town adjacent to Makabulos recounted how the Huk force spent the entire day prior to the attack infiltrating the area. Despite the brutality of the massacre, the local townspeople spoke of how well they had been treated by the Huks.

100. Ramon Magsaysay, Jr., interview with the author, Pasay City, Manila, 22 October 2012.

101. Ramon Magsaysay, Jr., interview with the author, Pasay City, Manila, 22 October 2012.

102. Greenberg, 70.

103. Greenberg, 88. See also Baclagon, 5, 7, and Macdonald, 142. On 26 July 1950 the Philippine Constabulary was brought under the Department of Defense by Executive Order No. 308. US military aid was contingent upon the merger. On 23 December 1950 Quirino published Executive Order No.

389, abolishing the major commands and activating a unified AFP structure consisting of the Philippine Army, Constabulary, Air Force, and Navy. It further divided the Philippines into four major area commands, with BCTs assigned to each area under a single unified command structure, which in turn was subordinate to the AFP Chief of Staff.

104. Charles T. R. Bohannon, Napoleon Valeriano, *Counter-Guerrilla Operations: The Philippine Experience* (Westport, CT: Praeger Security International, 2006), 103.

105. Kerkvliet, 208, 240.

106. The Chargé in the Philippines (Chapin) to the Secretary of State, 5 January 1951, *Foreign Relations of the United States, 1951*, 6, Part 2, 1491.

107. Cowen to US Embassy Manila, Department of State cable, 2 January 1951 (Myron Cowen Papers, Box 7, Truman Library, Independence, MO). Ironically, this exactly contradicts the assessment of *Chargé de Affairs* Vinton Chapin, who remarked in a telegram to the Secretary of State that Selga "is no stooge of Ramos." (The Chargé in the Philippines (Chapin) to the Secretary of State, 5 January 1951, 1492).

108. Ramon Magsaysay, Jr., interview with the author, Pasay City, Manila, 22 October 2012.

109. Due to security concerns Lansdale sought approval for Magsaysay to live with him on Camp Murphy. This close association is commonly cited in histories of the Huk campaign as a key source of Magsaysay's initiatives and as an example of the indirect control Lansdale exerted over Magsaysay.

110. Lansdale, *In the Midst of Wars*, 45-47.

111. Lansdale, 50-59. The Economic Development Corps, or EDCOR, was an initiative that provided plots of land, a carabao (water buffalo), building materials, and other essentials, to civilians, veterans, and reconciled Huks, on reclaimed government land. The first farm started in December 1950 and was activated in February 1951. The first farms were established in Mindanao, though others were later established in other parts of the country. A total of 25,000 Filipinos would benefit from the EDCOR initiative.

112. Lansdale, *In the Midst of Wars*, 47-48.

113. Office of the President of the Philippines, "Magsaysay Credo," Official Gazette of the Republic of the Philippines. http://www.gov.ph/1956/05/29/magsaysay-credo/ (accessed 18 November 2012).

114. Greenberg, 86. In its first year alone, this initiative received 59,000 telegrams, all of which received responses with three days.

115. Lansdale, *In the Midst of Wars*, 86.

116. The Chargé in the Philippines (Harrington) to the Department of State, 15 June 1951, *Foreign Relations of the United States, 1951*, 6, Part 2, 1547.

See also from the same volume, Memorandum Prepared by the Embassy in the Philippines, August 1951, 1562. Paradoxically, by helping to get the Philippine economy back on a positive track, thus forestalling economic disaster, the US reinforced the Quirino regime's power. Embassy officials were concerned that "we have developed a threat to the very institutions we wished to strengthen," and that Quirino's reinvigorated regime would seek "the elimination of the two-party system." These officials felt the best way to forestall this was by strengthening and encouraging the opposition Nationalista Party. However, their close association with the Quirino administration, a necessity for any diplomatic mission, alienated US officials from the opposition, further highlighting the diplomatic tight-rope officials were walking in the Philippines.

117. The Ambassador in the Philippines (Cowen) to the Department of State, 15 February 1951, *Foreign Relations of the United States, 1951*, 6, Part 2, 1506-1507.

118. Harold M. Vinacke, "Post-War Government and Politics of the Philippines," *Journal of Politics* 9, No. 4 (November 1947): 720. See also James L. Dalton, "Ins and Outs in the Philippines," *Far Eastern Survey* 21, No. 12 (30 July 1952): 122.

119. Lansdale, *In the Midst of Wars*, 90.

120. Macdonald, 157.

121. Nakano Satoshi, "Gabriel L. Kaplan and US Involvement in Philippine Electoral Democracy: A Tale of Two Democracies," *Philippine Studies* 52, No. 2 (2004): 153-155.

122. Lansdale, *In the Midst of Wars*, 90.

123. Lansdale, *In the Midst of Wars*, 91.

124. The Philippine Constitution authorized the establishment of an Electoral Commission that is responsible for administering, observing, and recording elections and their results. In 1950 the Philippine Congress passed legislation strengthening the electoral code. While the laws were on the books, this did not necessarily give the Electoral Commission the political strength to contend with the entrenched establishment, or the physical strength to supervise fair elections throughout the country. By law, the Electoral Commission could request the assistance of other government bodies in the execution of its duties. For a detailed description of the Electoral Commission see Vinacke, "Post-War Government and Politics of the Philippines."

125. Ramon Magsaysay, Jr., interview with the author, Pasay City, Manila, 22 October 2012.

126. Julian F. Harrington (Chargé de Affairs) to Cowen, 8 January 1952, Embassy Telegram, No. 2375 (Myron Cowen Papers, Box 6, Truman Library, Independence, MO).

127. Kerkvliet, 241.

128. "We Smashed the Communists: Philippine Leader Tells how Guns and Food Won War on Huks," *US News & World Report*, 13 February 1953 (Myron Cowen Papers, Box 12, Truman Library, Independence, MO), 35.

Chapter 4
New Threats

I was mortified by the excesses of high society at a time when poor people were still scrambling like mad.

> — Laurin B. Askew, interviewed by Charles Stuart Kennedy (1998).[1]

With the turn of the New Year in 1952, the Philippine government was making significant inroads against the Huks, largely thanks to the efforts of Ramon Magsaysay and his supporters, and Edward Lansdale and the US embassy team. Those inroads also represented potential problems. Though the people of Central Luzon were placing increased faith and trust in Magsaysay, that did not translate into faith and trust in the government. Despite empowering the electorate during the 1951 elections, politics in the Philippines and the political elites remained unchanged. Furthermore, by empowering the electorate, Magsaysay represented a threat to the entrenched establishment. The next two years would require even more unity of effort within the American team at the embassy and support from Washington, to counter Philippine establishment attempts to rid themselves of Magsaysay. The demands of the new situation required extraordinary insights into Philippine politics, society, and culture.

Ironically for the PKP and Huks, by late 1951 Magsaysay, someone *within* the government, was challenging the status quo and entrenched establishment. Through a policy of "all out force and all out friendship" Magsaysay was winning over the peasants that represented the Huks primary support base.[2] The new Secretary of National Defense was turning the situation around, combining genuine empathy with sociocultural understanding to gain popular support. Edward Lansdale ably supported Magsaysay in these efforts, providing ideas and the support required to see necessary reforms through to implementation. Despite the successes of 1950-1951 a long road lay ahead.

Just as the AFP was experiencing a renaissance under Magsaysay, the Huks were experiencing infighting and confusion amongst the ranks. Under PKP leadership, the Huks were ostensibly communist and subject to communist doctrine and theory, but outside of the senior leadership, the PKP-Huk union lacked theoretical and doctrinal depth. Unfortunately for the guerrillas, and fortunately for the Philippine government, the PKP leadership had not properly linked their ends with their means. The PKP wanted to install a communist government in Manila, while the agrarian peasant support they relied on did not share those aspirations.[3]

The PKP theoreticians and leadership espoused an early Soviet model of Bolshevism.[4] While few within the PKP and Huk movement had formally studied communism, leading men like Vicente Lava had actually studied in Moscow prior to World War II.[5] Under the Soviet model, the PKP preferred to focus on building support within the labor movement, ignoring the already rebellious peasants in Central Luzon for a significant amount of time. Though decidedly communist, Vicente Lava represented a more moderate track within the PKP. Internal divisions within the party promoted the fortunes of Vicente Lava's two younger brothers, Jose and Jesus. The elder Lava brother described his younger siblings as "intellectually arrogant, dogmatic, and sectarian, and liable to commit acts of serious leftist adventurism that would be irreparable."[6]

Leftist adventurism increasingly became the party's orientation after the capture of the Politburo in October 1950.[7] Unbeknownst to Magsaysay and Lansdale, that event had significant repercussions within the PKP-Huk leadership. Three men emerged as the new guiding lights of the PKP, Jesus Lava, Casto Alejandrino, and Mateo de Castillo.[8] Though well-grounded in communist theory, these men were all from wealthy families and preferred Manila to the countryside.[9] Throughout 1950 and 1951, the trio representing the Secretariat of the Politburo, developed policies that were increasingly out of touch with reality. Though the Huks had been on the rise in 1950 and were dealing significant blows to government forces, the PKP leadership failed to account for the AFPs evolution under Magsaysay.[10] Thus, as Huk fortunes took a turn for the worse, the PKP leadership continued to issue overly optimistic guidance based on outdated understanding of the situation.[11]

The Huk field commander, Luis Taruc, in attempts to clarify their orders and guide them toward more realistic objectives soon became a target of the Lava-Alejandrino-Castillo block.[12] Taruc advocated a "policy of self-preservation and conservation of our strength."[13] Though he had already been secretly removed as Huk military commander in August 1950, Taruc formally resigned the post during a PKP Central Committee conference in the spring of 1951.[14] Taruc was an extremely popular figure within the movement, representing the only member of the PKP-Huk senior leadership of peasant origin. His resignation suggests a radicalization of the party leadership and message just as radicalism was losing resonance with the masses.

It was after the Central Committee conference, when Lava, Alejandrino, and Castillo, advocated what was tantamount to full scale war that Taruc first started thinking that it might be time to come to terms with the government.[15] Taruc took an assignment with Huk Regional Committee 1, but continued to remain an extremely popular and influential figure within the Huk movement. The Lava-Alejandrino-Castillo Secretariat became increasingly insulated and isolated, preferring that "only those cadres that would offer blind obedience were to staff organizations working with them directly," and sending those who were out of favor to particularly dangerous Regional Committees, "where there was great danger of being isolated, captured, or killed."[16]

Just as the AFP was regaining popular support within the populace during the November 1951 elections, the Huks were preoccupied with internal matters. Instead of working to influence the elections, Luis Taruc was moving through the mountains of eastern Luzon during the first three weeks of November to join Regional Committee 1.[17] In the spring of 1952, Taruc and several other Politburo members held a local conference to discuss the 1951 Central Committee Resolutions in terms of the objectives specific to Regional Committee 1. The result of the conference was further Huk field force disillusionment with PKP leadership. However, any serious discussion within the PKP-Huk leadership that may have resolved these issues was hampered by increasingly effective AFP operations, constantly harrying Huk units.[18]

Prior to Magsaysay's reforms Philippine Army and Constabulary personnel were widely known for stealing food and other bare essentials from the populace, while the Huks were known for paying for everything they took. As AFP discipline improved under Magsaysay, these issues virtually disappeared. Additionally, improved AFP combat performance and operational planning forced the Huks away from their traditional support bases. When Huks were able to get into the barrios, the peasants no longer willingly offered support because of the improved relationship between the AFP and the populace, often forcing the Huks to use harsh and even terroristic measures to obtain the needed supplies.[19]

Improved combat performance and operational planning was not just a byproduct of Magsaysay's military reforms. As a former guerrilla, Magsaysay understood how the Huks operated, and remembering tactics the Japanese employed against his own guerrillas, he understood the fundamentals of countering the Huks.[20] Given the emotionally neutral definition of empathy, Magsaysay demonstrated that his empathy for the Huks informed his operations against them.[21] First and foremost though, he simply insisted that AFP and PC formations leave the safety of their garrisons and move into the jungles and hills to fight them on their own ground.[22] In Magsaysay's mind, the armed forces had to keep the Huks on the run. Based on accounts from former Huks, this tactic became increasingly successful, pushing some Huk units to the point of starvation.[23] The increased operational tempo also disrupted communications between the Huk squadrons, preventing any kind of coordinated response to AFP operations.[24]

Frequent offensive operations of increasing duration would have been pointless if the AFP and PC did not alter their earlier tactics of large scale sweeps. These operations provided the Huks ample warning of the armed forces intentions and usually resulted in little return for the amount of resources invested. Rather than large scale operations, Magsaysay emphasized smaller, intelligence driven operations. One officer from the period recounted how his unit spent countless hours conducting surveillance of local cemeteries for Huks attempting to visit their relative's graves.

> It took a lot of nonmilitary . . . call it, expertise, to do those things well. Because they don't teach those things in the military. You had to know not only personalities, but the way they operated, the way they related to their suspected relatives in the vicinity.[25]

A consequence of operations requiring significant local understanding, whether intended or not, was that when it came time to implement civic actions in that locality, the BCTs undoubtedly had much better understanding of the situation, allowing them to administer rehabilitation projects more effectively.

One small innovation that had a significant impact on the campaign was the creation of the scout ranger teams. The idea originated from a young Filipino lieutenant during one of the brainstorming sessions at Magsaysay and Lansdale's combined residence. Captain Rafael "Rocky" Ileto was a United States Military Academy graduate and had spent subsequent time in the US in ranger training.[26] He broached the idea of forming small teams of highly trained personnel who would take the fight into the heart of Huk territories.[27] These teams would conduct reconnaissance, raids, and ambushes in areas the Huks once thought secure. The scout ranger teams proved very effective during operations against the Huks, but they had a more important effect on AFP morale and aggressiveness. Rather than being isolated in a specialized organization, separate from the BCTs, each BCT had its own scout ranger team. As the regular soldiers of the BCT saw the successes of these small units against the elusive Huks, they were either shamed or emboldened to become more aggressive themselves, resulting in an overall improvement of individual BCTs as healthy competition developed between the line units and the scout ranger teams.[28]

Just as the scout ranger teams had a psychological effect on their fellow soldiers, Lansdale and Magsaysay wanted the AFP to have a psychological effect on the Huks. Complimentary to AFP offensive operations was the inclusion of psychological operations, or psywar as Lansdale referred to it, into some aspect of almost every AFP operation.[29] Lansdale was a strong advocate of psychological operations and helped establish a psychological warfare training center for the AFP.[30] While AFP offensive operations focused on attacking the Huks military strength, with casualties often the result, it appears the psychological operations focused more on Huk morale in an attempt to get them to surrender.[31] As noted previously, both men frequently cited the larger number of Huks who surrendered than were killed or captured, but as Magsaysay's thoughts on reconciliation demonstrated, he empathized with the Huk rank-and-file and preferred they rejoin society peacefully.

Without Magsaysay's security sector reforms the PKP may have been able to weather their internal divisions, because the underlying grievances of the peasants would have remained a legitimate recruiting tool. However, the success of the November 1951 elections in rebuilding popular faith in government, and increasing popular support for the AFP started to undermine peasant support, which was absolutely essential to the Huks. In September 1952 Taruc issued a "Call for Peace," that while continuing to espouse the PKP line, further divided Huks in the field and the PKP leadership.[32]

A House Divided

The internal PKP-Huk feuds could not have come at a better time for the Philippine government. Despite the positive effect the election had on popular confidence in democracy, it set the stage for conflict between Magsaysay and Quirino. The first fissures resulted from popular press coverage of the election, giving credit to the Secretary of National Defense. Quirino's vanity and ego were the first casualties in the conflict. "[Quirino] deplored this and all other insinuations that Magsaysay rather than Quirino was responsible for [the] honesty [of the] last elections. He contends that credit is due to him alone for the steps he took regardless of [political] consequences."[33] While Quirino might have been mollified following Magsaysay's media attention, the growing popularity and media coverage of Magsaysay's civic initiatives deepened Quirino's resentment.

The entrenched political establishment was growing increasingly hostile to Magsaysay as well. Magsaysay's arrest of Governor Eugenio Lacson over the Moises Padilla incident had already caused some alarm within elite circles. Additionally, the shake-up in congress caused by the 1951 election almost paralyzed the legislature, as committees and congressional leadership were constantly reshuffled in the first half of 1952. This drew the ire of the very power Speaker of the House, Liberal Party leader Eugenio Perez.[34] Perez was the representative and standard bearer of the Liberal Party old guard. Rather than watch the upstart Secretary of National Defense grow more powerful, Perez fueled fears of a Magsaysay initiated coup because of the latter's control over both the Philippine Army and Constabulary. Perez clamored for the return of the Constabulary to the Secretary of the Interior, a Quirino loyalist.[35]

Magsaysay's troubles were not confined to his own country either. In a memorandum from Myron Cowen to Lansdale in January 1952, Cowen relates a conversation with the Philippine Ambassador to the US, Joaquin M. Elizalde, in which the ambassador disparaged Magsaysay and planted rumors of impropriety.[36] Magsaysay's inspection tours had not diminished following the elections, and Quirino noted his frequent absences from cabinet meetings, questioning the motives as potentially political.[37]

Magsaysay's initiatives may not have been politically motivated at the time they were instituted, but they definitely developed his popular support base. By mid-1952, he was no longer a relatively obscure congressman from Zambales. His inspection tours, the 1951 elections, and the 10 centavo telegram program ensured he was virtually a household name. Lansdale noted that more and more people, of all walks of life were visiting Magsaysay at his quarters, and he "realized that, to the people, Magsaysay rapidly was becoming *the* government, *the* leader who cared about what was happening to them and who would try to right any wrongs."[38] By the fall of 1952, popular feelings were not simply confined to visitors to Magsaysay's quarters. During trips into the provinces, Lansdale noted overwhelmingly positive public reaction to Magsaysay in areas that had once been solidly Huk territory.[39]

Part of that positive public reaction stemmed from an increased respect for the rule of law within the AFP. Despite advocating for and receiving a suspension of the writ of habeas corpus, Magsaysay reassured US officials he would not engage in the typical abuses associated with such a move.[40] It appears that Magsaysay was good to his word. According to former President Fidel Ramos, a junior officer in the AFP during the Huk campaign, "you [could not] just apprehend people…you must develop information, until finally you have a legal basis for apprehending."[41] Despite broad powers to prosecute the Huk campaign, Magsaysay reversed the previous trend of the campaign that ignored civil rights.[42] This approach further demonstrated to the masses that someone within the government was attempting to alter the status quo.

Filipino civilians were not the only ones Magsaysay appealed to and won over. In addition to the AFP reforms, Magsaysay developed an effective reconciliation and reintegration program for surrendered Huks. Though he may not have had the benefit of modern counterinsurgency doctrine, which stresses the importance of reconciliation programs, Magsaysay saw the issue in terms of healing the rifts in Philippine society.[43] Magsaysay and Lansdale both made frequent reference to the number of Huks who surrendered compared to the number of killed or captured as an example of the effectiveness of their campaign.[44] Once cleared of any civil criminal acts, the Huks were inducted into the AFP as a way to demonstrate their allegiance to the government and dedication to democracy.[45] In Magsaysay's opinion, the majority of the Huk rank-and-file "never were Communists really. They were just desperate men."[46] By providing an acceptable alternative to the Huks, Magsaysay was not only winning away popular support of the populace, he was beginning to win away Huk manpower.

Secretary Magsaysay believed the hard-core communists within the Huks had to be destroyed militarily, but rehabilitation remained his main course of action for the rest.[47] Magsaysay took an interest in the cases of individual Huks, as mentioned earlier in his son's recounting the case of Eddie Ngolab, and also in the accounts of Carlos Romulo and Lansdale.[48] Magsaysay's desire to rehabilitate in hopes that other Huks would surrender upon hearing of the good treatment afforded other surrendered Huks took its toll on the Huk movement. As Luis Taruc recounted, "the new discipline he imposed within the army, his good public relations, and his treatment of Huks who surrendered or had been captured and who were willing to turn over a new leaf, seriously threatened the morale of our rank and file."[49]

Arguably the most often cited example of Magsaysay's rehabilitation policy was the EDCOR program. Though widely publicized, EDCOR only resettled around 300 Huk farmers and their families.[50] However, numbers were not Magsaysay's concern. Though Lansdale may have intended to use EDCOR for its psychological value, Magsaysay saw it as building new communities in which the former Huks would rejoin society by working alongside fellow Filipinos.[51] The secretary's ideas were not simply aimed at defeating the Huks, but at rebuilding society. Significant resources went into the EDCOR project generating some criticism about the cost in view of the small return, but as a subordinate of Magsaysay noted, the cost was ancillary because the real purpose of EDCOR "was to create communities."[52]

In the summer of 1952 the situation in the Philippines was secure enough for Magsaysay to travel to the United States in an official capacity. His last trip resulted in the Americans backing him as Secretary of National Defense. The 1952 trip reaffirmed US faith in Magsaysay as the right man for the job. In meetings with officials at both the Departments of State and Defense, Magsaysay received praise. Yet the visit raised concerns in certain Philippine government circles. In a letter from Myron Cowen to Philippine Ambassador to the US, Carlos Romulo, Cowen reassured him that "their sole interest in him is as a man who is honest and courageous and intensely interested in cleaning up the Huks and bringing peace and order back to the Philippines."[53]

Though American intentions had not yet coalesced around Magsaysay as a potential candidate for the presidency, Lansdale was already thinking and planning along those lines. Edward Lansdale's team, code named Kugown, continued to focus on defeating the Huks militarily, while he found ways to promote his friend.[54] In conjunction with Magsaysay's trip to Washington, Lansdale engineered an invitation by the International Lions Club to Magsaysay to be the key-note speaker at their conference in Mexico City in June 1952. Under intense pressure from all sides, including his own daughter, Quirino gave Magsaysay approval to speak at the event. Quirino was wary of the event because of the notoriety it would afford Magsaysay, and he suspected Lansdale of orchestrating the invitation.[55] The affairs surrounding the 1951 elections alerted the entrenched political establishment to Lansdale's efforts, and by the summer of 1952, Quirino was increasingly hostile towards the American.

Despite the 1951 election results the embassy was finding it increasingly difficult to work with Quirino and the entrenched political establishment. In 1952 Quirino was already eyeing the 1953 presidential election, and was more than reluctant to push the land reform necessary to alleviate continuing social tensions.[56] Amongst existing politicos in Manila, US officials determined that "neither Quirino or Lopez in the Liberal Party, nor Laurel or Recto in the Nationalista Party, have shown the slightest indication of taking any interest in land reform."[57] The only real leverage the Americans had was military aid, and if they withheld that aid it would potentially reverse recent AFP military successes, just when the Huks were looking weakest.[58]

Fortunately, embassy leadership, in the form of Ambassador Raymond Spruance and Counselor William Lacy, had a grasp on the situation, understanding the necessity of Lansdale's plans.[59] However, a number of key positions continued to be staffed by "China hands" that made the mistake of "thinking that the rest of Asia was like China."[60] Lansdale provides more clarity about the US mission in the Philippines.

The US civilian mission, polarized on the Embassy, operated almost as though the Huk fight didn't exist, except as a conversation piece and its battlegrounds being places to avoid. There were exceptions to this general attitude, of course, notably the Ambassador and several of his chief assistants."[61]

In light of this, Lansdale's team continued to focus on getting into the provinces to see conditions for themselves. In September 1952, Lansdale sent one of his most trusted subordinates, Charles T. R. Bohannon on a shadowy reconnaissance mission into the Bicol region of southeaster Luzon.[62] The purpose of the reconnaissance was to ascertain the suitability of Bicol for "friendly" guerrilla operations, as opposed to an anti-Huk campaign.

By late 1952 the Philippines were a flurry of political activity. In an attempt to co-opt Magsaysay's popularity, Quirino offered him the vice-presidency if he would be his running mate in the 1953 election. Magsaysay was opposed to the idea out of principle, and turned him down.[63] Beyond the principle, Quirino would be able to marginalize Magsaysay as vice-president, and deprive him of his main source of power, the AFP.[64] Following the rejection, US embassy officials suspected Quirino of engaging in intrigue to determine Magsaysay's next move. The situation was so sensitive that Ambassador Spruance and William Lacy ceased sending sensitive cables by traditional means, opting instead to send handwritten letters to Washington, suspecting Quirino was monitoring their message traffic.[65]

Nationalista Party leaders seized the opportunity almost immediately. They approached Magsaysay quietly to offer him the presidency on the Nationalista ticket. Part of their rationale was that with Magsaysay on the ticket, the AFP would not be used against them during the election.[66] Ambassador Spruance was skeptical of Nationalista Party leadership, believing their motives to be dubious. He was concerned that they would use Magsaysay's popularity during the campaign season, and then drop him from the ticket just before the election. Without the backing of the Nationalista Party apparatus, it would be extremely difficult, if not impossible for Magsaysay to win on his own. The embassy was equally concerned about Quirino's reaction if he discovered that Magsaysay had secretly agreed to side with the Nationalistas. William Lacy believed that if Quirino felt sufficiently threatened, he might resort to authoritarian measures, such as declaring martial law, or jailing political opponents.[67]

The Liberal Party establishment attempted to hedge their bets by making veiled threats to US officials in Manila. In mid-December 1952 a Quirino loyalist, Senator Macario Peralta paid an unannounced call on Ambassador Spruance and charged embassy personnel with directly interfering in Philippine politics. He specifically cited Lansdale and James D. Bell, a political officer in the embassy. Spruance subsequently informed the State Department that "I desire to emphasize this [message is] not to be construed as [a] reflection [on] either Lansdale or Bell, both of whom I regard as outstanding men who have not stepped outside the limits of their duties and instructions." Spruance assessed that Quirino and Liberal Party leadership were behind the visit and that they hoped the threat of public attacks in the press would be sufficient to get the embassy to back away from calls for free elections and reforms.[68]

In the response from the State Department, Deputy Secretary of State David Bruce suggested that Lansdale's presence was no longer required in the Philippines and that he should return to the US immediately. Lansdale was already due to return to the US on leave, but Spruance informed the State Department that his presence in the Philippines was essential because of his contacts and influence with Magsaysay, and he should be allowed to return to the Philippines.[69] Upon returning Lansdale soon found himself without a home. Following a meeting with Filipino officials, JUSMAG chief Major General Albert Pierson answered a reporter's question in such a way that Lansdale was publicly no longer welcome in the JUSMAG.[70] Reassigned to the 13th Air Force's office of the historian at Clark Air Base north of Manila, Lansdale continued to covertly run Magsaysay's campaign. Regardless of his new cover, Quirino and his associates now watched Lansdale more than ever.[71]

The impetus for the final split between Quirino and Magsaysay came on 27 February 1953, when the President told reporters that Magsaysay was "only good for killing Huks."[72] Magsaysay response clearly indicated a much deeper appreciation of the problems facing the Philippines and their potential solutions:

It would be useless for me to continue as Secretary of National Defense with the specific duty of killing Huks as long as the administration continues to foster and to tolerate conditions which offer fertile soil for Communism. Merely killing dissidents will not solve the Communist problem. Its solution lies in the correction of social evils and injustice, and in giving the people the decent government free from dishonesty and graft.[73]

However, Quirino's statement also provided the perfect cover to allow Magsaysay to resign ahead of the planned Nationalista Party convention scheduled for March. During the convention, the party would announce Magsaysay as their candidate for president.[74] With the announcement of Magsaysay's candidacy, all eyes turned to the elections in November, clouded by memories of the 1949 elections.

Significance of November 1953

There was little disagreement by anyone about the importance of the 1953 elections. Quirino and the Liberal Party saw the election as either an opportunity to reinstate the status quo ante, or the end of their monopoly on power. The Huks most likely saw it as an opportunity to keep Magsaysay out of power and further undermine popular confidence in the government. The Americans and the opposition, led by Magsaysay, saw it as the opportunity to keep the democratic process alive in the Philippines.[75] All of the progress made against the Huks could be undone if the 1953 elections went the way of the 1949 elections.

Even before Magsaysay resigned as Secretary of National Defense, US officials were cautioning him about what it would mean once he lost control of the military.[76] Almost immediately, Magsaysay and his family were forced to leave the protective environs of Camp Murphy (AFP headquarters in Manila), and for the next seven months the family took up residence with various friends.[77] Magsaysay's successor as Secretary of National Defense, Oscar Castello, proved to be a Quirino loyalist and no friend of Magsaysay. Magsaysay's supporters quickly experienced run-ins with Castello's men during any kind of public assembly, and the clashes escalated into what could almost be described as open warfare between the two groups.[78] Without the Philippine security forces at his disposal, Magsaysay was increasingly vulnerable.

Though Magsaysay did not control the military officially, he still had a considerable number of loyalists within the AFP. The two main loyalist groups appear to have been former guerrillas and reconciled Huks.[79] Magsaysay's support base in the AFP represented a paradox for the United States. The AFP made significant strides in professionalization under Magsaysay, but a crisis that forced the AFP to choose between loyalty to the government and loyalty to a man could undermine those strides. A State Department committee established to assess the 1953 election's implications determined that significant violence was quite possible if Quirino managed to engineer a victory similar to that of the 1949 election.[80] Lansdale's own assessment of the situation, in his after action report to the CIA about the elections, was more severe, "if the Liberals had robbed the election there would have been a revolution, led by Magsaysay."[81] Complicating matters was the growing belief that even if Quirino won a clean election there would still be violence.[82]

Magsaysay broached the subject with US officials, but they counseled against such a course of action.[83] A Magsaysay led revolt would likely have split the AFP in two, with Magsaysay's supporters within the military turning their weapons on Quirino's loyalists, led by the still intact AFP old guard Magsaysay had been unable to completely expel as Secretary. The pro-Quirino forces would not have been insignificant, and if Quirino won a relatively fair election, his forces would still be the recipients of significant US military aid. Based on this, the US had to make its position absolutely clear to Magsaysay, President Quirino, and the Liberal Party.

A potential Magsaysay led revolt that risked splitting the AFP in two raised difficult questions. As mentioned earlier, the US took significant risk in backing a man who was capable of developing widespread popular support and loyalty. He managed to professionalize the AFP in terms of its responsibility to act in the best interests of the people rather than self-interest, improve its tactical and technical proficiency, and rejuvenate morale and *esprit de corps* within the ranks. Yet in a Western-style democratic government, the armed forces are loyal to the constitution rather than a certain political party or individual. Many within the AFP upheld their oaths to the constitution during the 1951 election, some of them at great professional risk.[84] However, the context of the situation had changed. Magsaysay was now a political candidate, outside of the recognized government, rather than their official leader. In the 1951 elections, upholding their oaths to the constitution implied doing the right thing, whereas in 1953, the same act implied the opposite. The risk to long-term AFP professionalism and apoliticism highlighted the importance of not only a fair election in 1953, but a Magsaysay victory as well.

As soon as Magsaysay was viewed as a viable candidate, US officials analyzed their policy options. The problem for the Americans was that while supporting Magsaysay was clearly in their best interests, they could not be seen as intervening in Philippine domestic politics. Yet it was virtually impossible for the US not to become involved in Philippine domestic politics. Even without overt statements of US support, those politicians viewed as having the support of the Americans, and thus able to receive increased aid, had a decided advantage over their opponents.[85] The US had to tread carefully with Magsaysay. As Deputy Secretary Bruce noted in his cable to Ambassador Spruance, the US-Magsaysay relationship already threatened to derail US-Philippine relations, and that full support for Magsaysay's Huk campaign was far different than support for him as a candidate against the administration he was serving in. In Bruce's view, "any widespread conviction that he is hand-picked candidate of US [would] not further his own [political] career."[86]

Bruce elaborated that US policy "operates on [the] basis [of] principles rather than personalities." Finally, Ambassador Spruance was to emphasize that Filipino politics was the sole business of Filipinos and that "people [should] continue to choose leaders they desire in free and honest elections; that we will cooperate with any [non-communist] administration so elected." He believed that the press and others would conclude that "although we will never so specifically state, that [administration] which comes into power thru force and corruption will not receive US [military] and [economic] aid."[87] Ironically, by stating that the United States would only cooperate with a non-communist government, and that an administration elected through coercion would not receive aid, Bruce was advocating intervention.

Such a policy may seem decidedly neutral, but it was clear to all involved that by supporting a policy of free and fair elections the US was warning the Quirino administration. The embassy staff understood the policy to mean "supporting free elections in the Philippines was support to Magsaysay."[88] In order to avoid discovery of US intervention, support for Magsaysay had to come from Lansdale's team, with peripheral assistance from embassy assets.[89] Covert actions in support of Magsaysay in 1953, while more diverse and widespread, were patterned on the model established during the 1951 elections.

From Secretary of National Defense to President

In Lansdale's opinion, if the US was going to defeat communism in the Philippines they had no alternative but to support Magsaysay's campaign. He believed that "with a government brought into being by the power of the people and reflecting their will in its actions, the people would deeply resent and oppose any attempt at armed overthrow of that government (their government) by the Communists."[90] Lansdale had no doubt that Magsaysay would succeed in a fair election against Quirino, and directed his efforts and those of his team toward ensuring a fair election. However, they faced an entrenched elite that were shocked and dismayed that the lower classes actually wanted to vote as they pleased.[91]

The first step was organizing Filipino political support behind Magsaysay. While the Nationalista Party political machinery was a necessary evil for Magsaysay, he would need support from trusted non-American advisors. As an opposition candidate to the sitting president, Magsaysay could no longer seek council from those he once did, like William Lacy and Ambassador Spruance. Lansdale did not have to work hard to find men of character to help Magsaysay. Senator Lorenzo Tañada of the Citizen's Party and Eleuterio "Terry" Adevoso, the founder of the Hunter's ROTC Guerrillas during the war, were two well-connected politicians who quickly offered their services. Additionally, the Papal Nuncio of the Philippines, Signor Emilio Vagnozzi, lent support to the Magsaysay campaign through the Catholic Church's voter education program, Catholic Action.[92]

In addition to the specific individuals mentioned by Lansdale, Magsaysay enjoyed the support of the Philippine Junior Chamber of Commerce, Lions Club, and Rotary Club.[93] These organizations could not only support Magsaysay's campaign, as chapters of worldwide organizations they could leverage international support. Magsaysay also had the support of the Philippines Veterans Association, an organization he had once been a provincial president in, and one that had extensive grassroots access and support.[94] Lastly, Magsaysay's ability to garner the loyalty of his subordinates ensured that the men who had served as his protection detail as Secretary of National Defense, joined him on the campaign trail after resigning from the AFP.[95] This would prove extremely important, as Lansdale became increasingly suspicious of the security personnel assigned to Magsaysay by the government.[96]

With trustworthy support in place, Lansdale's team reinvigorated the organizations they built for the 1951 election, and built relationships with other groups to diversify their outreach. Lansdale's subordinates worked hard to ensure NAMFREL played an even bigger role during the 1953 election than it did in the 1951 election. The result was that the organization "gained strength in the first half of 1953, emerging prior to election day as a highly respected national body (candidates and citizens alike turned to it for impartial help)."[97] The Committee for Good Governance, an organization started for the 1951 election, was revived to act as an intermediary with foreign press correspondents, ensuring they were present at polling sites. Finally, the Magsaysay for President Movement, "a group of business and professional people . . . headed by Terry Adevoso" was active in building grassroots support for the candidate.[98] By the time of the election the MPM had chapters in 15,600 of the approximately 18,000 barrios in the Philippines.[99]

The press played an important role in the 1951 elections, and Lansdale was intent on repeating that successful relationship with a useful ally. Using his vast contacts within the Philippine press establishment, Lansdale was able to garner support from many of the major publications. Through a trusted, longtime friend and supporter of Lansdale's efforts in the Philippines, Manuel "Manny" Manahan, they were able to prepare the Philippine News Service to act as election watchers on election day.[100] The Americans also established their own newspaper, The Free Philippines.[101] The paper operated underground during the Japanese occupation, and reviving it for the election was a calculated psychological move to rekindle popular memories of resistance. Their publication also served a secondary function of providing the Americans valuable intelligence on the situation in the provinces, as they were increasingly forced to keep a low profile during the campaign.

Lansdale's preparations for the election and support for Magsaysay's campaign focused on educating the populace and ensuring a fair election. "All of our major efforts . . . went into teaching Filipino people to stand up by themselves and work as free men. This was in keeping with our consistent operating philosophy of helping the Filipinos to help themselves."[102] It also reflected his empathetic personal belief that the Filipino people were engaged in a righteous struggle that America was duty-bound to support.[103] He believed that if he could achieve those two objectives, Magsaysay was capable of winning over the electorate. Early reaction to Magsaysay's resignation and speculation of his nomination resulted in such widespread support that Ambassador Spruance speculated that if the election had been held in April 1953 he would have easily won. However, he went on to caution that it would "undoubtedly be tough and dirty."[104]

Lansdale was correct to believe in Magsaysay's ability to win over the electorate. He oriented his energetic campaign toward connecting with the common man.[105] "By November, he probably will have shaken the hand of every voter in the country...and they love it."[106] He seemed to be made for the campaign trail and impromptu, unscripted meetings with the people. As Secretary of National Defense Magsaysay often spent time with local peasants during his inspection tours to get a sense of what they were experiencing, but this was likely limited to where there AFP was operating. Now that he was a presidential candidate those constraints were lifted. Magsaysay engaged with the electorate everywhere he went, and though he was campaigning, he took the time to stop and connect with individual Filipinos.[107]

Magsaysay was criticized for his poor public speaking ability earlier in his career, likely stemming from his poor mastery of English and preference for native Filipino dialects.[108] However, in a letter from Lansdale to Cowen about the campaign, he informed Cowen that "you would thoroughly enjoy the way friend Ramon campaigns. You recall what a lousy public speaker he is. Well, he's knocking around in the barrio circuit in jeeps, trucks, caratelas, and carabao carts mostly shaking hands with people and talking only a few minutes." He continues by noting it is "simple stuff, sure, but the people eat it up, understand it, and feel that here is one of them – far more than the big words that [Carlos Romulo] uses or the "economic mobilization" words of Quirino."[109]

If Magsaysay was the embodiment of a young, energetic candidate, Quirino was the exact opposite. The president's health had never been good, but it took a turn for the worse during the campaign, leaving Philippine and US government officials speculating about what would happen if Quirino died. Vice President Jose Yulo was "quietly running the government from behind-scenes in Malacañan."[110] In a display of his deep sociocultural understanding, Lansdale further related the political intrigues taking place in the event of Quirino's death:

> [Romulo] and Lopez say privately that they will quickly hold another Liberal convention and get the [Liberal Party] to back their ticket. Yulo, though, is now a deadly enemy (probably will destroy the Lopez clan politically in July or August) and probably would inherit Quirino's file of material to keep politicos (such as Perez) in line.[111]

Even with Quirino in poor health, the Liberal Party machinery was hard at work behind trying to preserve their grip on power. The files mentioned above were the dossiers compiled by Antonio Quirino's own semi-official agents, and with the election in full swing they were being used towards other ends.

In 1947, President Roxas had formed a special intelligence division within Malacañan that answered solely to the president, and under the command of former guerrilla leader Marcos "Marking" V. Agustin. A US Army counterintelligence corps report on the unit noted that the agents carried weapons, had badges and credentials, but lacked any real training and experience in traditional intelligence gathering operations. The investigator also noted that many of the agents had criminal records and had been brought up on charges of abuse of authority.[112] When Roxas died and Quirino assumed the presidency, he inherited the organization.

Antonio Quirino wasted no time getting to work. One of his targets was Lansdale, but the poor training of the agents was evident in Lansdale's immediately associating them with Quirino:

> Your old buddies Tony Quirino and the Markings (Yay and Agustin) are in our hair plenty. Tony has got himself recalled to active duty as a Lt-Col and is running a lot of intelligence service activities out of General Duque's office. Agents are mostly Marking's boys.[113]

Their amateurish methods included phone taps, surveillance, and an occasional attempted ambush that never achieved the intended purpose.[114]

What concerned Lansdale more than Quirino's agents were his overtures towards the Huks. "What worries me is that Tony has been playing footsie with Luis Taruc; the latter hopes to play the Moscow peace line and arrange an amnesty again; Tony wants the Huks out of the hills and working hard for the Liberal ticket in central Luzon."[115] Taruc sent his son Romeo as emissary to Quirino with assurances of safe passage by Antonio Quirino and Chief of Staff of the Army, General Calixto Duque.[116] As Romeo Taruc relates the story, he was taken to a meeting at the home of Speaker of the House Eugenio Perez. Unbeknownst to Taruc, Perez, Duque, and the Quirino's, the driver sent to pick up Romeo was a Magsaysay loyalist. Rather than reaching his destination he was taken to the prison at Camp Murphy. Romeo Taruc went on to explain that Quirino was afraid of Magsaysay so he was willing to negotiate with the Huks.[117]

Quirino also attempted to use the AFP to Liberal Party advantage. Throughout 1953, Quirino loyalists were hard at work preparing for the election. By October, two-thirds of PC provincial commanders had been replaced by Quirino loyalists, officers known to oppose use of the AFP for political purposes were transferred to non-command assignments, and speculation was rampant that Quirino would install a new Secretary of National Defense and AFP chief of staff.[118] Ironically, the results of Quirino's meddling would likely have weakened the AFP in the long term. If he won the election through fraud, he would either have faced a revolt by Magsaysay loyalists or a resurgent Huk movement which would reap the benefits of popular disillusionment with democracy. In either event, the very instrument he would need to defeat these threats would have been weakened in order for him to attain his goal.

In addition to Quirino's manipulation of the AFP, he sought to directly tamper with the ballots. During the election, the individual responsible for tallying the votes was the provincial treasurer. In July and August, the most trustworthy treasurers were called to Manila to work on the national budget for the next fiscal year, with "acting" treasurers appointed, "who follow orders."[119] Despite US covert and diplomatic activities to ensure a fair election, Quirino's actions to secure a Liberal victory by any means transformed the election into something more significant. "Rumors of a recurrence of the violence and dishonesty characteristic of the Presidential election four years ago have given the forthcoming elections the character of a test of representative government in the Philippines."[120]

For all of Quirino's schemes, Lansdale still achieved his goal. In November 1953, the Filipino people elected Ramon Magsaysay President of the Philippine Republic by an overwhelming majority: 2,912,992 to Quirino's 1,313,991.[121] The US-Filipino team dedicated to Magsaysay's election accomplished the task by teaching and encouraging the populace; encouraging government agencies and departments to uphold their sworn duties instead of bowing to political pressure; physically protecting Magsaysay from threats; ensuring fraud and corruption were quickly publicized; working closely with the press; keeping tabs on Liberal Party activities; and leveraging the significant talent residing within the embassy team.[122] Where the Americans and Magsaysay's team leveraged the legitimate political process,

> The Liberal Administration campaigned using the old Spanish and Malayan system of working with leaders (family heads, village elders) as well as the American system of ward bosses. The people simply changed age-old customs, stopped following normal leaders, [and] acted each for himself. This was the real revolution which took place.[123]

Magsaysay's supporting team was able to alter the political status quo by leveraging his enormous popularity to overcome the entrenched establishment. The establishment had relied on a system that had not accounted for someone like Magsaysay.

The Presidency

Ramon Magsaysay assumed office in late December 1953, and a short time later Edward Lansdale returned to the United States, his mission in the Philippines complete.[124] The fight against the Huks and for Philippine democracy was not yet over for Magsaysay. As president he had to live up to the reputation he developed as Secretary of National Defense and while on the campaign trail. This would prove no easy task in the face of a political establishment that was still controlled by many of the same men who represented the system Magsaysay wanted to overthrow, some within his own party.[125] The one thing Magsaysay could count on in the near term was the electorate. His enormous victory, as mentioned above, clearly gave him a popular mandate, and building on the empathy he had developed for the lower classes, he was intent on living up to the people's expectations.

Magsaysay's first actions were in keeping with his personality and character.[126] During the campaign he promised the people that he would open the doors of Malacañan to the public. After his inauguration he returned to the Palace and expected to find Filipino citizens joining him to see the historic palace. When he found the doors still locked, because a member of his staff wanted to give him time to rest after the inauguration, he got angry and demanded the doors opened immediately.[127] Magsaysay wanted to be around the people who had elected him president. As Frisco San Juan affectionately remembered of his former leader, "the people always…he would be lonely without the people."[128]

As average citizens were seeing the grounds of the presidential palace for the first time, Magsaysay was attempting to bring a degree of transparency to the government. On 5 January 1954, he issued an executive order, requiring all public servants to make their financial records open to the public. Magsaysay led the way by making his own records public on 3 January 1954. The order required compliance by 31 January 1954.[129] He announced this measure through his Press Office, which was going into overdrive to keep up with Magsaysay's activities. The Press Office began issuing almost daily press releases on everything from Magsaysay's day to day activities, to details of Huk surrenders, to abuses of public office by government officials.[130] With one instrument, Magsaysay was humanized for the average Filipino, the people could track the progress of the campaign against the Huks, and they could see what their own officials held accountable for their actions.

Continuing a program Magsaysay started as Secretary of National Defense, he reinstituted the 10 centavo telegram that worked so well previously. To cope with the volume of telegrams his office received, Magsaysay established the Presidential Complaints and Action Commission (PCAC), appointing Manuel Manahan as its first director. The PCAC was no longer focused just on the Huks or AFP abuses, it encompassed the entire government. Every government agency was answerable to the PCAC.[131] The program was so successful that Magsaysay's staff established a radio show to publicize the work performed by PCAC on behalf of Filipino citizens.[132]

Despite all of his presidential duties, Magsaysay continued to take a personal interest in the problems of his people. Frisco San Juan, who would take over as the second director of the PCAC, recalled a time when Magsaysay was supposed to attend a conference with AFP and other government officials. Instead of attending the conference he took his own car to Nueva Ecija province to check on the status of a complaint filed by a farmer claiming his landlord beat him.[133]

Magsaysay's campaign against the Huks culminated shortly after taking office. In February Magsaysay instructed Manuel Manahan and Benigno Aquino, Jr. to open negotiations with Luis Taruc to try to convince him to surrender. On 16 May 1954, Taruc surrendered to Aquino. Taruc's son Romeo noted his father's weariness at seeing Filipino's killing Filipino's, and Taruc's own writing suggests exhaustion as a primary cause of his surrender.[134] However, Magsaysay and Lansdale's operations had also reduced the Huk support base to almost nothing, and Huk fighters were surrendering in ever increasing numbers because of the lure of Magsaysay's reconciliation policies.

All of the programs and initiatives described thus far demonstrate Magsaysay's desire to remain as closely connected to the people as he had ever been. In Magsaysay's mind "it's a leadership issue. He's from them. He's with them. And he's out to help them out."[135] People saw Magsaysay as different. He was not one of the "professional politicians" and was unlike all the previous presidents.[136] Unfortunately for Magsaysay, the professional politicians and their political machines were still very much opposed to some of the policies he had promised during his campaign.

Despite the popular mandate Magsaysay received from the Filipino people in November 1953, he still faced opposition from congress and entrenched elites. In the opinion of knowledgeable US officials, party leadership from both sides would likely "oppose any radical departure from conservative economic policies and will probably have more political influence than the group favoring a liberal point of view."[137] The uneasy union of Magsaysay with the Nationalista Party was embodied in the relationship between the new president and party leader Claro Recto. "[Magsaysay] distrusts and fears Recto but both emotions are colored by a great respect long since acquired for Recto's intellectual attainments and his remarkable powers of political improvisation . . . Recto's attitude toward [Magsaysay] is one of thinly disguised condescension."[138]

On one side was Magsaysay and his supporters, "mostly AFP men plus some talented amateurs like Manny Manahan," while the other side consisted of the old guard of the Nationalista Party and certain business interests.[139] While Magsaysay's opponents were opposed to land reform, they were able to compromise in certain areas, and the president was determined to work around the issues his own party was presented him:

> He had executive initiatives on community development. So he worked within the scope of the executive. He would issue executive orders. On those . . . the congressmen and senators knew he was trying to help the poor, so they did not really bother blocking him. They were very supportive, except on the land reform. They wanted him blocked.[140]

Even in the face of stiff opposition from his own party, Magsaysay continued to push for the social and land reform issues he had promised the Filipino electorate during his campaign.[141] However, popular support of the masses did not necessarily translate into political capital in Manila.

The level of US support Magsaysay enjoyed from 1950-1954 virtually evaporated overnight. Absent the PKP-Huk menace, US policy makers no longer felt the need to push for reforms behind the scenes. The Eisenhower administration had already shifted focus to the communist threat in Vietnam, generally leaving Magsaysay and the Philippines to fend for themselves.[142] Lansdale's departure for Vietnam, along with a significant number of his CIA team members, created a void that appears to have never been filled. The effect of this policy shift away from the Philippines was felt in Washington. "We would go into a National Intelligence Estimate (NIE) meeting and there would be 40 people in the room. Not many of those 40 knew a lot about the Philippines."[143] This was only a few years after the Philippines had been a major theater in the war against communism in Asia, and was still far from being socially and politically stable.

Despite the challenges Magsaysay faced during his two and a half years as president, he and Lansdale succeeded in two very important tasks. First, the Huks ceased to be an existential threat to the Philippine government, and stability in general. As the representative voice of one faction within the PKP-Huk movement, Luis Taruc noted in 1954 that they viewed Magsaysay's administration differently than the Quirino administration. The people had spoken in the 1953 elections and it was time to seek peace.[144] Second, and related to the first success, the popular support generated by Magsaysay for the government restored its legitimacy in the eyes of the electorate. Instead of being the focal point of peasant and lower class outrage and derision, the government was now perceived as responsive to their needs. Magsaysay and Lansdale's success was further highlighted by the fact that they were able to accomplish those rather significant feats in only four years, in the face of opposition from both an armed insurgency and an entrenched establishment.

Notes

1.   Laurin B. Askew, Economic Officer, Manila (1954-1956); interviewed by Charles Stuart Kennedy (1998), ADST/CRS.

2.   Fidel V. Ramos, interview with the author, Makati City, Manila, 22 October 2012.

3.   Kerkvliet, 265. While religion in general, and Catholicism particularly, was a factor, the existing literature does not suggest that it was a significantly divisive issue, as the PKP tended to avoid the question of religion. Philippine-US efforts to capitalize on the doctrinal communist stance on religion likely encountered the same problem the PKP experienced in their attempts to indoctrinate the lower classes. The majority of people simply either did not care about or understand the ideology. They were merely fighting back against a repressive government and unacceptable societal conditions. Intellectual appeals from both sides were lost because the PKP had long since given up on preaching the ills of religion to their rank-and-file. Because so few of the rank-and-file did not understand communist doctrine to begin with, Philippine-US psychological operations highlighting the communist stance on religion likely fell on deaf ears. Thus, it appears that the Huk rank-and-file generally retained their largely Catholic identity throughout the campaign.

4.   Fidel V. Ramos, interview with the author, Quezon City, Manila, 15 October 2012.

5.   Kerkvliet, 103. Vicente Lava was a well-known Filipino scientist who had actually served in the Philippine government's Bureau of Science and held a doctorate from Columbia University. According to Lansdale, only about seven Filipinos went abroad to study communism, with five going to the Soviet Union and two going to China. He contrasts this with the dozens of Vietnamese who studied in the Soviet Union and China, citing this as one of the reasons why the Vietnamese communists were so much stronger than their Filipino counterparts. This may also explain why the PKP espoused Marxist-Leninist doctrine as opposed to Maoist, despite the larger agrarian base extant in the Philippines at the time (Lansdale, *A Comparison: Viet Nam and the Philippines*, 3-4).

6.   Luis Taruc, *He Who Rides the Tiger* (New York: Frederick A. Praeger, 1967), 95.

7.   Based on the context of Vicente Lava's statements, "leftist adventurism" might be characterized as the radical leadership of the PKP attempting to infiltrate and subvert other social and labor groups and movements in order to bring them under PKP domination. This is as opposed to Taruc and Vicente Lava's view that the best hope for political and social change in the Philippines was through a broad based coalition, or united front, representing the interests of many diverse groups. Leftist adventurism, as suggested by Taruc, was heavily influenced by Leninist principles, and also sought the armed overthrow of the government, just at a time when he believed the PKP-Huk movement was not militarily capable of such a move.

8. Taruc, *He Who Rides the Tiger*, 92.

9. Kerkvliet, 100.

10. Taruc, *He Who Rides the Tiger*, 97.

11. Taruc, 109. Among the more unrealistic objectives set forth by the Secretariat in the 1951 Central Committee Resolutions were to "establish revolutionary local governments and peasant committees for the distribution of land, to levy revolutionary taxes, and to create revolutionary workers' committees in all key industries and public utilities in the country."

12. According to Romeo Taruc, in an interview with the author, 18 October 2012, the break between Taruc and his colleagues during the 1951-52 period persists to this day in the form of separate Huk veteran's organizations, the Huk Foundation, and the Hukbalahap Veterans Association.

13. Taruc, *He Who Rides the Tiger*, 98.

14. Taruc, 93.

15. Romeo Taruc, interview with the author, Angeles City, Pampanga, 18 October 2012.

16. Taruc, *He Who Rides the Tiger*, 98-99.

17. Taruc, *He Who Rides the Tiger*, 103-104.

18. Taruc, 121.

19. Kerkvliet, 237.

20. "We Smashed the Communists," 32, 35.

21. As defined in Chapter 1, empathy is "the ability to experience and relate to the thoughts, emotions, or experience of others."

22. William Pomeroy, *The Forest* (New York: International Publishers, 1963), 102-103, 138, 190. See also Karnow, 668.

23. Pomeroy, 123-137, 210-211, 228-230, 233-234.

24. Romeo Taruc, interview with the author, Angeles City, Pampanga, 18 October 2012.

25. Fidel V. Ramos, interview with the author, Makati City, Manila, 22 October 2012.

26. Lansdale, *In the Midst of Wars*, 49. Ranger operations of the time were characterized by small unit actions focused on long range infiltrations of the enemy lines to conduct ambushes, raids and sabotage. In the case of an insurgency, the concept simply meant that rather than infiltrating enemy lines, the small units infiltrated into insurgent controlled areas to conduct the same types of operations.

27. Edward Lansdale, "A Case History of Insurgency: The Philippines," lecture, National War College, 25 March 1964 (Lansdale Papers, Box 74,

Hoover Institution Archives, Stanford University, Palo Alto, CA). The culminating "exercise" for scout ranger candidates, prior to graduating, consisted of infiltrating a known Huk stronghold and returning alive, either with useable intelligence or a confirmable report that they had eliminated the Huks in the area.

28. Lansdale, *In the Midst of Wars*, 50.

29. Lansdale, 71.

30. Lansdale, 70.

31. Lansdale, 75-78. While the operation associated with this citation is simply one example of the many types of psychological operations employed by the AFP, throughout the available sources it is clear that the vast majority of these types of operations were meant to encourage Huks to surrender, whether through enticement, sowing suspicion amongst the Huk ranks, coercion, or playing on popular local superstitions. For a comprehensive account of the psychological operations employed by the AFP during the Huk campaign, see Chapter 5 of Lansdale's autobiography, *In the Midst of Wars*.

32. Taruc, *He Who Rides the Tiger*, 122.

33. Julian F. Harrington (Chargé de Affairs) to Cowen, 8 January 1952, Embassy Telegram, No. 2375.

34. H.M. Menzi to Cowen, personal correspondence, 5 May 1952 (Myron Cowen Papers, Box 5, Truman Library, Independence, MO).

35. Robert S. Hendry (Associate Editor, Philippines Free Press) to Cowen, personal correspondence, 4 December 1951, (Myron Cowen Papers, Box 9, Truman Library, Independence, MO).

36. Official Memorandum for Melby and Lansdale from Cowen, 8 January 1952, declassified, (Myron Cowen Papers, Box 6, Truman Library, Independence, MO). Since departing Manila as the US Ambassador to the Philippines, Cowen had assumed duties in Washington, DC, as the Consultant to the Secretary of State on Far Eastern Affairs and Special Assistant to the Secretary of State for Mutual Security Affairs.

37. Ramon Magsaysay, Jr., interview with the author, Pasay City, Manila, 22 October 2012.

38. Lansdale, *In the Midst of Wars*, 101.

39. Lansdale., 101.

40. Macdonald, 151.

41. Fidel V. Ramos, interview with the author, Makati City, Manila, 22 October 2012.

42. Cliff Forster interview.

43. Romulo, Gray, 142, 174. For modern counterinsurgency doctrinal references to reconciliation programs see Headquarters, Department of the Army, *Field Manual 3-24.2: Tactics in Counterinsurgency* (Washington, DC: Government Printing Office, 2008), 4-11, 7-5, 7-7, 7-8, and US Government Counterinsurgency Guide January (Washington, DC: Bureau of Political-Military Affairs, 2009), 3, 15, 23. For United Kingdom Ministry of Defense doctrinal references see Ministry of Defense, *Army Field Manual: Countering Insurgency*, vol. 1, part 10, January 2010, p.1-13.

44. Lansdale, *In the Midst of Wars*, 51. See also, "We Smashed the Communists: Philippine Leader Tells how Guns and Food Won War on Huks," 32. According to Philippine Army records cited by Lansdale in his autobiography, "6,874 Huks were killed and 4,702 were captured, while in the same period *9,458 Huks surrendered*!" Magsaysay cites similar (rounded) figures in his interview with US News & World Report.

45. "We Smashed the Communists," 32.

46. "We Smashed the Communists,", 35.

47. Romulo, Gray, 142.

48. Romulo, Gray, 142-143. According to Romulo and Gray's account, a surrendered Huk named Amat was guilty of three murders, but Magsaysay felt he had acted out of desperation and wanted to give him a second chance. Magsaysay provided a small machine shop in the prison so he could earn a living, in hopes that Amat's story would entice other Huks to surrender. For Lansdale's account see *In the Midst of Wars*, 51. In Lansdale's account, a Huk named Tomas Santiago "had approached Magsaysay with the intent of killing him, only to lose heart and surrender." Once in prison Santiago wanted to redeem himself, and Magsaysay eventually provided him wood and tools so he could resume his former trade as a carpenter. As other prisoners saw what was happening, they wanted the same opportunity. Eventually, Magsaysay had their carpentry shop incorporated as a business. The ex-Huk carpentry firm later bid on, and won, a contract to make furniture for the AFP.

49. Taruc, *He Who Rides the Tiger*, 97.

50. "We Smashed the Communists," 32.

51. Fidel V. Ramos, interview with the author, Makati City, Manila, 22 October 2012.

52. Ramos.

53. Myron Cowen to Carlos P. Romulo, personal correspondence, 26 July 1952 (Myron Cowen Papers, Box 7, Truman Library, Independence, MO).

54. Edward Lansdale under pseudonym "Geoffrey Villiers," *The Philippines Election, 1953*, 23 November 1953 (Lansdale Papers, Box 34, Hoover Institution Archives, Stanford University, Palo Alto, CA). Lansdale allegedly chose his codename for the operation by randomly selecting a name from a phone book (Karnow, 665-666).

55. Romulo, Gray, 163-166.

56. The Ambassador in the Philippines (Spruance) to the Secretary of State, 8 September 1952, *Foreign Relations of the United States, 1952-1954*, 12, Part 2, (Washington, DC: Government Printing Office, 1987), 498.

57. Spruance.

58. Spruance.

59. Lansdale, *In the Midst of Wars*, 104-105. Lansdale describes Spruance and Lacy's support as critical for garnering Washington's approval for his plans for the 1953 elections.

60. James J. Halsema, Information Officer, USIS, Manila (1952-1954); interview by G. Lewis Schmidt (1989), ADST/CRS.

61. Lansdale, *A Comparison: Viet Nam and the Philippines*, 23.

62. Charles T. R. Bohannon, *Report of Reconnaissance of the Bicol Region, September 1952*, declassified, (Bohannon Papers, Box 28, Hoover Institution Archives, Stanford University, Palo Alto, CA).

63. Ramon Magsaysay, Jr., interview with the author, Pasay City, Manila, 22 October 2012.

64. The Ambassador in the Philippines (Spruance) to the Department of State, 1 April 1953, *Foreign Relations of the United States, 1952-1954*, 12, Part 2, 523-524. Additional reasons outlined for Magsaysay turning Quirino down are the President's refusal to guarantee free elections and institute political and administrative reforms; that it would not make sense to run for vice-president when he could run for president; Magsaysay's popular standing threatened Quirino; and Magsaysay would have to work within the Liberal Party apparatus, which was run by Eugenio Perez, and Magsaysay would find "association with Perez almost unbearable." Perez had enormous political power and he and his "cronies" support was absolutely essential to Quirino.

65. The Counselor of Embassy in the Philippines (Lacy) to the Assistant Secretary of State for Far Eastern Affairs (Allison), 31 October 1952, *Foreign Relations of the United States, 1952-1954*, 12, Part 2, 508-510. In one instance, Magsaysay came to William Lacy's office to tell him that he had overheard President Quirino telling men close to him that he wanted to use the Philippine military to ensure a Liberal Party victory in the 1953 elections. Lacy suspected that Quirino's "slip," making those statements in Magsaysay's presence, was really an attempt to 1) know who Magsaysay was meeting with at the embassy, 2) determine Magsaysay's relationship to Nationalista Party leadership, 3) determine embassy attitude toward a Magsaysay candidacy, 4) if evidence could be adduced, request removal of Ambassador Spruance and/or Lacy, and 5) make Magsaysay out to be a US tool or puppet.

66. Ramon Magsaysay, Jr., interview with the author, Pasay City, Manila, 22 October 2012.

67. Memorandum for the Assistant Secretary of State for Far Eastern Affairs (Allison), 5 December 1952, *Foreign Relations of the United States, 1952-1954*, 12, Part 2, 515.

68. The Ambassador in the Philippines (Spruance) to the Department of State, 10 December 1952, *Foreign Relations of the United States, 1952-1954*, 12, Part 2, 520.

69. The Ambassador in the Philippines (Spruance) to the Department of State, 10 December 1952, 520.

70. Currey, 120. As will be noted in more detail in the last chapter of this thesis, the relationship between Major General Pierson and Edward Lansdale requires additional research. In the specific case of Lansdale's return to the Philippines it is unknown if Pierson played any part in spurring the initial call from Washington for Lansdale's departure from the Philippines, and subsequent reservations about his return. By early 1953, the Office of Policy Coordination was no longer under the combined purview of the Departments of State and Defense, and was solely under the control of the CIA. Without departmental ownership of Lansdale's mission it is possible that complaints and appeals from Pierson may have found a receptive audience in both departments.

71. Lansdale to Cowen, declassified personal correspondence, 11 June 1953, (Myron Cowen Papers, Box 6, Truman Library, Independence, MO).

72. Currey, 119.

73. Hart, 69.

74. The Ambassador in the Philippines (Spruance) to the Department of State, 31 December 1952, *Foreign Relations of the United States, 1952-1954*, 12, Part 2, 526.

75. Ramon Magsaysay, Jr., interview with the author, Pasay City, Manila, 22 October 2012.

76. The Ambassador in the Philippines (Spruance) to the Department of State, 31 December 1952, 526.

77. Ramon Magsaysay, Jr., interview with the author, Pasay City, Manila, 22 October 2012.

78. Frisco San Juan, interview with the author, Quezon City, Manila, 15 October 2012.

79. Frisco San Juan.

80. Memorandum for the Assistant Secretary of State for Far Eastern Affairs (Allison), 16 December 1952, *Foreign Relations of the United States, 1952-1954*, 12, Part 2, 524.

81. Lansdale, *The Philippines Election, 1953*, 6. Lansdale discounted the rumors at first, but gave them more credence when individuals associated with Magsaysay and others associated with the 1949 Batangas Revolt approached

his team and other US officials with specific requests for items like anti-tank weapons.

82. Memorandum for the Assistant Secretary of State for Far Eastern Affairs (Allison), 16 December 1952, 523.

83. Buell, 452. US officials were in a difficult position with the revelation that Magsaysay was considering leading an armed revolt against Quirino. Magsaysay and Lansdale, with the assistance of JUSMAG, made great strides in professionalizing the AFP in a short time. Ironically, that professionalism was supposed to translate into loyalty to the constitution and the nation rather than patrons or political parties, i.e. Quirino and other politicians. Loyalty to Magsaysay rather than to the constitution would demonstrate that the AFP had not truly professionalized, but instead found a more palatable patron.

84. Lansdale to Lavinia Hanson (Valeriano), personal correspondence, 5 March 1984.

85. Memorandum by the Officer in Charge of Philippine Affairs (Wanamaker) to the Director of the Office of Philippine and Southeast Asian Affairs (Bonsal), 5 December 1952, *Foreign Relations of the United States, 1952-1954*, 12, Part 2, 518. In 1946, Manuel Roxas was perceived to be General MacArthur and High Commissioner Paul McNutt's choice for president. In 1949, Quirino was perceived to be Ambassador Cowen's choice for president over the collaborationist Jose Laurel.

86. The Acting Secretary of State to the Embassy in the Philippines, 13 December 1952, *Foreign Relations of the United States, 1952-1954*, 12, Part 2, 521.

87. Acting Secretary of State, 522.

88. Robert L. Nichols, Branch Public Affairs Officer, USIS, Davao (1951-1954); interviewed by Robert Amerson (30 August 1988), ADST/CRS.

89. Earl Wilson, Public Affairs Officer, USIS, Manila (1950-1952); interviewed by G. Lewis Schmidt (1988) ADST/CRS.

90. Lansdale, *The Philippines Election, 1953*, 1.

91. Charles J. Nelson, Public Administration Specialist, International Cooperation Administration (ICA), Manila (1952-1955); Special Advisor to Mission Director for Rural Development/Deputy Chief, ICA, Manila (1956-1958); interview by Celestine Tutt (1981), ASDT/CRS. During a trip to the provinces Mr. Nelson encountered the matron of a large estate, and she talked "about the persons who worked on her estate. She was talking about the fact that the farmers wanted to vote as they pleased. She was really upset about this."

92. Lansdale, *The Philippines Election, 1953*, 2. Terry Adevoso, Frisco San Juan, and Jaime Ferrer founded NAMFREL for the 1951 elections with Lansdale's support.

93. The Counselor of Embassy in the Philippines (Lacy) to the Assistant Secretary of State for Far Eastern Affairs (Allison), 31 October 1952, 509.

94. Frisco San Juan, interview with the author, Quezon City, Manila, 15 October 2012.

95. Frisco San Juan. See also, Romulo, Gray, 197. This demonstration of loyalty, though admirable under the circumstances, called into question the future viability of the AFP as an apolitical organization. Mr. San Juan's earlier quote about the role of hero worship in Philippine society highlights the issues that a popular figure like Magsaysay raised. Fortunately, Magsaysay was a man of principle and character, who actively sought counsel before acting.

96. Lansdale, *The Philippines Election, 1953*, 2.

97. Lansdale. Signor Vagnozzi was already well known by Quirino, as the President had tried to have the Vatican recall him. The US Embassy intervened on his behalf by contacting the Archbishop of New York, Cardinal Francis Spellman to relay their concerns to the Vatican (Assistant Secretary of State for Far Eastern Affairs (Allison) to the Counselor of Embassy in the Philippines (Lacy), 2 December 1952, *Foreign Relations of the United States, 1952-1954*, 12, Part 2, 513).

98. Lansdale to Cowen, declassified personal correspondence, 11 June 1953.

99. Gosnell, Harold F. "An Interpretation of the Philippine Election of 1953." *The American Political Science Review* 48, no. 4 (December 1954): 1135.

100. Lansdale, *The Philippines Election, 1953*, 2.

101. Lansdale, 3. The Free Philippines was published by Manuel Manahan, with the aid of Juan "Johnny" Orendain and others.

102. Lansdale, *The Philippines Election, 1953*, 4.

103. Lansdale to Cowen, declassified personal correspondence, 11 June 1953.

104. The Ambassador in the Philippines (Spruance) to the Department of State, 6 March 1953, *Foreign Relations of the United States, 1952-1954*, 12, Part 2, 529-530.

105. Frisco San Juan, interview with the author, Quezon City, Manila, 15 October 2012.

106. Lansdale to Cowen, declassified personal correspondence, 11 June 1953.

107. Luz Magsaysay to Dorothy Cowen, personal correspondence, 10 September 1953 (Myron Cowen Papers, Box 6, Truman Library, Independence, MO). See also Macdonald, 167. Also Frisco San Juan, interview with the author, Quezon City, Manila, 15 October 2012.

108. Romulo, Gray, 89-90, 95, 98. Carlos Romulo was one of those who noted Magsaysay's gaffs while Secretary of National Defense during his visit to Washington, DC in 1952. Ambassador Cowen and Lansdale both shared those concerns. It is likely that Lansdale's claim that his team wrote most of Magsaysay's major speeches originates from their earlier concerns. However, previous Filipino politicians utilized Americans as speech writer; for example, Julius Edelstein served as President Roxas' speech writer until the formers departure, as noted by Lansdale in his journal (previously cited).

109. Lansdale to Cowen, declassified personal correspondence, 11 June 1953. The cartellas and carabao carts mentioned by Lansdale are traditional Philippine modes of transportation. A caratella is generally a small, two-wheeled, horse, mule, or donkey drawn, covered carriage. A carabao cart is similar to a caratella, but is often uncovered and is drawn by a carabao, which is a type of water buffalo.

110. Lansdale to Cowen, declassified personal correspondence, 11 June 1953.

111. Lansdale.

112. 229th Counterintelligence Corps Detachment, Captain Paul R. Lutjens, PHLRYCOM, *Malacañan Intelligence Division*, 7 February 1949 (Bohannon Papers, Box 28, Hoover Institution Archives, Stanford University, Palo Alto, CA).

113. Lansdale to Cowen, declassified personal correspondence, 11 June 1953.

114. Lansdale.

115. Lansdale.

116. Taruc, *He Who Rides the Tiger*, 126.

117. Romeo Taruc, interview with the author, Angeles City, Pampanga, 18 October 2012.

118. Memorandum Prepared for the Ambassador in the Philippines (Spruance), 2 October 1953, *Foreign Relations of the United States, 1952-1954*, 12, Part 2, 549. According to this source, "an unsigned handwritten note on the source text" stated that Lansdale prepared the memorandum. Other actions by the Quirino administration and Liberal Party cataloged by Lansdale and the embassy staff included recalling the most honest provincial treasurers to Manila to work on the next year's budget, and replacing them with compliant acting treasurers. Provincial treasurers are responsible for receiving municipal ballot tallies, compiling them into a provincial tally, and reporting the provinces ballot results to the Electoral Commission. Liberal Party officials also attempted to pressure managers of the Philippine National Bank "to refuse crop and developmental loans to selected persons opposing the Liberals." The Liberals also attempted to use the tax collection services to make "sudden demands

for taxes or sudden reallocation of land…these means have been used, also, in keeping Liberal rank-and-file in line." Liberal candidates were also taking control of municipal mayors and police forces in certain localities to assist in fraud during the election. The Liberal Speaker of the House, Eugenio Perez was believed to have been distributing blank ballots to officials in the provinces for use on election day. A courier who was bringing samples of the fraudulent ballots was believed to have been murdered while traveling to Manila with the samples. Government officials were also believed to have hired 800-1,000 "goons" by October 1953, but the number was expected to dramatically increase on election day. Among the "goons" were the "intelligence agents" of the Office of the President mentioned previously (Memorandum Prepared for the Ambassador in the Philippines (Spruance), 2 October 1953, 550-551).

119. Memorandum Prepared for the Ambassador in the Philippines (Spruance), 2 October 1953, 549.

120. Memorandum by the Under Secretary of State (Smith) to the Executive Secretary of the National Security Council (Lay), 16 July 1953, *Foreign Relations of the United States, 1952-1954*, 12, Part 2, 539.

121. Currey, 130. The combined voter turnout of 4,226,983 was out of a total population of roughly 18 million in late 1953.

122. Lansdale, *The Philippines Election, 1953*, 4-7. In reference to protecting Magsaysay, Lansdale specifically mentions one incident in which the Kugown team sanctioned a direct action operation by security forces loyal to Magsaysay after receiving intelligence that a man named Ben Ulo was in command of a group of men President Quirino had recently released from prison, all of whom were serving life sentences for murder. These men were to ambush Magsaysay during a campaign stop in Pangasinan, and Lansdale's team sent messages to Magsaysay to cancel the trip. Magsaysay went anyway in order to support an embattled local politician. Lansdale's team "marshaled all security forces" with one specific mission, "to get Ulo first. Ulo disappeared. The ambushes did not take place."

123. Lansdale, 9. Lansdale's reference to "ward bosses" is actually a reference to the traditional Philippine political process of the time. Under the traditional system a congressional candidate from a certain party would nominate mayoral candidates for each of the towns in his province. The mayoral candidate would then nominate municipal councilors and barrio lieutenants. In return for those nominations, the barrio lieutenants were expected to deliver votes for the mayoral candidate, who then delivered votes for the congressional candidate. If the province was controlled by the presidential candidate's party, those votes would also carry over to the presidential candidate (Bungaard, 279).

124. Currey, 132-133.

125. Bungaard, 280-281.

126. Romulo, Gray, 31. One of Magsaysay's first actions was to officially change the spelling of the presidential residence from the English spelling, Malacañan, back to the Tagalog spelling, *Malcañang*.

127. Frisco San Juan, interview with the author, Quezon City, Manila, 15 October 2012.

128. Frisco San Juan.

129. Office of the Press Secretary, "RM Orders Gov't Officers, Employees Bare their Finances; Abolishes IB," Press Release No. 1-6-3, 6 January 1954, (Lansdale Papers, Box 34, Hoover Institution Archives, Stanford University, Palo Alto, CA).

130. Office of the Press Secretary, Unnumbered Press Release, 3:30 pm, 4 January 1954 (Lansdale Papers, Box 34, Hoover Institution Archives, Stanford University, Palo Alto, CA).

131. Office of the Press Secretary, "President Appoints Crisol Acting NBI Director," Press Release No. 1-4-2, 4 January 1954 (Lansdale Papers, Box 34, Hoover Institution Archives, Stanford University, Palo Alto, CA).

132. Office of the Press Secretary, "PCAC Press Release," Press Release No. 2-4-3, 4 February 1954 (Lansdale Papers, Box 34, Hoover Institution Archives, Stanford University, Palo Alto, CA).

133. Frisco San Juan, interview with the author, Quezon City, Manila, 15 October 2012. When Magsaysay arrived in Nueva Ecija he investigated the incident and found that the landlord in question had actually been a "heavy contributor" to his presidential campaign. Regardless of the contribution, Magsaysay ordered the landlord arrested when he saw evidence of the landlord's beatings.

134. Romeo Taruc, interview with the author, Angeles City, Pampanga, 18 October 2012.

135. Ramon Magsaysay, Jr., interview with the author, Pasay City, Manila, 22 October 2012.

136. Alfredo Lim, interview with the author, Manila City Hall, 22 October 2012.

137. Memorandum by the Deputy Director of the Office of Philippine and Southeast Asian Affairs (Day) to the Deputy Assistant Secretary of State for Far Eastern Affairs (Drumright), 16 November 1953, *Foreign Relations of the United States, 1952-1954*, 12, Part 2, 558.

138. Untitled memorandum regarding the situation in the Philippines, 10 March 1954, (Myron Cowen Papers, Box 6, Truman Library, Independence, MO).

139 . Untitled memorandum.

140. Ramon Magsaysay, Jr., interview with the author, Pasay City, Manila, 22 October 2012.

141. Petzel, 91-92. See also Bugaard, 280; Macdonald, 180. In 1954, Magsaysay successfully pushed through Congress the Agricultural Tenancy Act, which codified the regulations for "share and leasehold rentals." A year later he successfully passed the Act Creating a Court of Agrarian Relations. Later that year he also passed the Land Reform Act of 1955. Also in 1955 Magsaysay successfully made the positions of mayor and municipal councilor elected positions for ten chartered cities; previously, these positions were by presidential appointment.

142. Macdonald, 173, 180.

143. Stephen Low, Philippine Affairs, Bureau of Intelligence and Research, Washington, DC (1956-1957); interviewed by Professor I.W. Zartman (1988), ASDT/CRS.

144. Kerkvliet, 247.

Chapter 5
Conclusion

> Violence takes much deeper root in irregular warfare than it does in regular warfare . . . It becomes very difficult to rebuild a country, and a stable state, on a foundation undermined by such experience.
>
> — Sir B. H. Liddell Hart, *Strategy*.[1]

The US-Philippine government campaign against the Huks from 1946-1954 offers important insights into limited US intervention on behalf of a foreign government. The lessons of the campaign may not have appeared relevant to counterinsurgency practitioners and policy makers during the US-led campaigns in Iraq and Afghanistan because of the scope of operations in those countries, thus precluding significant analysis of the Huk campaign. However, the Huk campaign may provide important lessons for future interventions and serve as a critical comparison for operations in Iraq and Afghanistan going forward.

Ramon Magsaysay and Edward Lansdale successfully executed a counterinsurgency campaign against the Huk movement because of their shared empathy, deep sociocultural understanding of the Filipino people, and their complimentary capabilities and resources. The evidence clearly suggests that Magsaysay's programs and initiatives, and Lansdale's covert operations, demonstrated their empathy and sociocultural understanding, but would have been impossible without their complimentary capabilities and resources.

Lansdale and Magsaysay's empathy for the Filipino people originated from their frequent contact with the Filipino people, particularly those in the provinces, and interaction with the Huks themselves. Magsaysay's empathy was critical to the success of the Huk campaign for several reasons. First, it allowed him to fill the paternalistic void extant in Philippine society at the time. Amidst the social dislocation following World War II the Huks started to fill the void left by an unresponsive upper class. Had the trend continued unchecked, the relatively localized Huk movement may have grown into a wider societal conflict bordering on civil war.

Second, Magsaysay's empathy aided him in rapidly rebuilding the morale and *esprit de corps* of the armed forces. In his role as Secretary of National Defense, Magsaysay served a paternalistic function for his soldiers. Where they had no advocate before, now the Secretary himself was taking a genuine interest in their welfare. In little more than a year Magsaysay had a profound impact on the armed forces. The AFP Magsaysay inherited in the fall of 1950 was hardly visible in the AFP that secured the clean elections of 1951.

Lansdale's empathy was critical to the eventual success of the campaign because people perceived him as genuine and trustworthy. These characteristics allowed him to develop the wide network of contacts throughout Philippine society that informed his actions during the campaign. Without these contacts and access to Philippine society, Lansdale may have gone in one of two directions. He might have resigned himself to the same benign insularity that so many other Americans in the Philippines seemed content to accept. The other, and perhaps worse, course he might have taken was one of arrogance and belligerence, coercing his Filipino counterparts into implementing ill-informed programs and initiatives. Lansdale's empathy also provided a solid foundation for his relationship with Magsaysay, which was characterized by mutual trust and respect.[2] Without this foundation it is unlikely that their association would have lasted long. If Lansdale had not trusted or respected Magsaysay, the counterinsurgent camp probably would have polarized between the Americans and Filipinos because of the deep respect, trust, and loyalty Magsaysay's followers had for him.

Magsaysay and Lansdale demonstrated sociocultural understanding in the types and design of the programs, initiatives, and covert operations they executed. They understood that in a counterinsurgency campaign local governance breaks down, offering the insurgents an opening to exploit, and that "the man in uniform whether he is a policeman, a constabulary man, or an army trooper [becomes] the sole link between the government and the masses, or the governed."[3] Understanding this, they were able to select the programs, initiatives, and covert operations that would have the most effect on the population and the Huks. Even the smallest military operations against the Huks usually incorporated psychological operations grounded in sociocultural understanding. Rather than focusing just on improving the combat capabilities of the AFP, they also spent considerable time developing the AFPs popular image. Lansdale and Magsaysay understood that the existing image when they took over the campaign reinforced the popular perception that the whole government was against the people.

Lansdale's covert operations in support of Magsaysay clearly demonstrated his sociocultural understanding. He understood that Magsaysay would become a threat and therefore a target of the entrenched political and social elites. Lansdale's operations and the support of US officials at the embassy were specifically calculated to provide Magsaysay the necessary time to implement his programs and initiatives and see results. Specifically, he understood that in Magsaysay lacked support from the powerful political clans in the Philippines. In order to prevent Quirino from removing the upstart Secretary of National Defense, popular opinion and support for Magsaysay was absolutely necessary.

The complimentary capabilities and resources of Lansdale and Magsaysay allowed them to execute the programs, initiatives, and covert operations that removed the Huks as an existential threat to the Philippine government. Magsaysay's son noted that while Lansdale provided his father with "a lot of guidance on counterinsurgency," Magsaysay, Sr. in turn showed Lansdale "the way it should be done . . . in the Philippines."[4] Lansdale also provided Magsaysay valuable political guidance about operating at the national level, while Magsaysay proved to be the catalyst needed to repair Philippine society. Lansdale and his team initially worked with Magsaysay under the impression they were building him up, but they quickly realized that he was a force all his own. Lansdale came to understand that while he could manufacture an image, he could not manufacture a man.

Lansdale derived his authority from his parent organizations, the Office of Policy Coordination and the Central Intelligence Agency. Magsaysay's power and authority were derived from the popular support of the people, not just his governmental positions. Interestingly enough, neither man abused that authority. Historians and political scientists may disagree about the degree to which Lansdale interfered in the domestic politics of the Philippines. However, Lansdale's actions simply empowered the Philippine electorate through free and fair elections. As noted by most observers of the time popular disgust with the existing regime almost guaranteed popular support for Quirino's opposition in 1951 and Magsaysay in 1953.

When distilled to its essence, the counterinsurgency campaign in the Philippines represented an extremely effective ends-ways-means analysis on the part of both men. Lansdale and Magsaysay determined the proper ends, i.e. the objectives of their programs and initiatives, because of their empathy for the people. They determined the proper ways to accomplish those objectives through deep sociocultural understanding. Finally, their complimentary capabilities and resources served as the means for accomplishing their objectives.

Critics might argue that the Huk campaign was not truly successful because communism was not eradicated, and Huk remnants gave birth to the New People's Army. However, the Huks did not really give birth to the New People's Army; unaddressed social, political, and economic grievances rejuvenated a popular support base for the communists. Thus, the Philippine government allowed a communist resurgence, where it had previously only been a nuisance after 1954. Magsaysay's untimely and tragic death in 1957 prevented full implementation of the reforms that might have permanently relegated the communists to nuisance status. Of note, Magsaysay became a measure of character and integrity for future Filipino leaders.[5]

Lansdale may have been able to help manufacture the image of Magsaysay, but he could not, and did not have to, manufacture the man that was Magsaysay. After Magsaysay's death, US officials, particularly those in the CIA, were quick to start looking for "another Magsaysay."[6] While there may have been candidates of similar caliber available, it appears as though American officials settled for regimes more closely resembling Quirino's than Magsaysay's. The communists no longer represented an existential threat to a "democratic" Philippine government. As long as Philippine policies were in line with American policy there was no reason to continue pushing for reforms that strengthened democratic institutions and further alleviated social unrest. The ascension of Ferdinand Marcos in the 1960s and US policy toward his regime in subsequent years highlighted America's return to schizophrenic Philippine policy. It is perhaps no small coincidence that US policy toward the Marcos regime only shifted once the Cold War in Asia had largely subsided.

Subjects of Further Study

The psychological effects of World War II, the Japanese occupation, and the subsequent Huk rebellion, on the Filipino population deserve further study. Numerous Filipinos from the period cited the population's experiences during the occupation, as the reason for the moral and ethical decay of Philippine society.[7] Murder, torture, rape, and robbery topped a long list of crimes that became common place from 1942-1945. As one contemporary observer of the time noted "the war made it seem that to obey was to abandon the good fight, while to resist the law was heroic."[8] Historical texts tend to catalogue the atrocities committed on both sides of the conflict, rather than analyze the long-term social and cultural implications of the irregular war that raged in Central Luzon during the occupation. As a former member of the Hunters Guerrillas noted "at the age of 21 in my area, I had the power of life and death."[9] Such power and authority proved difficult to relinquish for many of the guerrillas. The post-war Huk rebellion may very well emerge as simply the second phase of a civil war that began during the occupation, and continued until the people regained faith in the central government.

The existing scholarship would be thoroughly complimented if the lives of Luis Taruc and Ramon Magsaysay were compared and contrasted in the context of occupation guerrilla activities and the Huk rebellion. Their lives possessed striking similarities. Taruc and Magsaysay were both "of the people" in that they came from the barrios.[10] Both men came from humble financial origins and managed to impress their bosses with their character and integrity, earning them promotions.[11] Both men courted women from wealthy families and encountered upper class discrimination in the process.[12] They were also capable of imbuing profound loyalty in their subordinates, and became extremely popular leaders.[13] Once in positions of power and authority they faced political opposition, Magsaysay's coming from the entrenched political establishment, and Taruc's coming from the largely urban intellectual elites of the PKP.[14] A study of these two men would provide a unique look at the entire period from the perspective of two of the most important participants.

Another important relationship requiring additional research and illumination was that of Lansdale and Major General Albert Pierson. Lansdale maintained good relationships with two of the three JUSAMG chiefs during his service in the Philippines, but had a decidedly negative relationship with Pierson. Despite the fact that Pierson and Lansdale were at odds during a critical period of the Huk campaign, 1952-1953, very little has been written about that relationship. Pierson was the Assistant Division Commander of the 11th Airborne Division during the liberation of the Philippines, and the division was cited by Americans and the Huks as having had a positive relationship with the Huk squadrons in their area of operations.[15] With that background, Pierson could have been an asset during the counterinsurgency campaign. Yet he actively worked to remove Lansdale from JUSMAG and may have gone behind Ambassador Spruance's back, to officials in Washington, to have Lansdale removed from the Philippines altogether. Without understanding all of Pierson's background it is difficult to ascertain his motives.[16] If Pierson was indeed going behind Ambassador Spruance's back to work for Lansdale's removal, an in-depth study of that relationship could have wider implications for the subject of unity of effort within embassy teams, and between Washington and US officials abroad.

An important, though unanswered, question was whether or not the US had a contingency plan if Quirino won a fraudulent election in 1953, causing Magsaysay to initiate or join an armed revolt against the government. US policy clearly linked fair elections with future economic and military aid, but Quirino's actions during the 1953 campaign indicated that future aid was secondary to short-term regime survival. If Quirino won a victory reminiscent of 1949, and Magsaysay and his supporters responded with violence, the US government would have been in a precarious position. Backing Quirino would have likely destroyed any future relationship with the opposition and would fuel communist propaganda both in the Philippines and internationally. If America backed the opposition they would have been directly interfering in the domestic affairs of a government they once supported, which also could have fueled communist anti-imperialist propaganda. Though US officials in the Philippines were confident of Magsaysay's victory given a fair election, they must have given significant thought to alternate outcomes. Identifying an American contingency plan would go a long way towards determining the degree to which Magsaysay's election was a "no fail" mission.

Finally, further research of the differences between Lansdale's operations in the Philippines and those in Vietnam may provide insights into the pitfalls of using the same campaign model in two vastly different environments. Lansdale may have been a victim of his own success. Immediately after completing his work in the Philippines, he went on to Vietnam and embarked on a counterinsurgency campaign partnered with President Ngo Dinh Diem. His failure there led some of his former colleagues in the Philippines to conclude that "Ed got along fine with Filipinos, but he didn't understand the Vietnamese."[17] It is difficult to comprehend how a man who was so successful at connecting on a personal level with Filipinos from all walks of life, was unable to do the same in Vietnam. As this paper has shown, Lansdale's ability to connect on that personal level was instrumental in shaping his operations in the Philippines. Further research and comparison of his operations in the Philippines and Vietnam would clarify where Lansdale actually failed in the latter country.

Enduring Conclusions

The Huk counterinsurgency campaign demonstrates that limited intervention on behalf of a sovereign state is possible. A significant caveat to this statement is that while limited, the US was still heavily invested in the campaign behind the scenes. Even junior officials at the US embassy understood they "were involved in nation-building in a very real sense."[18] However, this statement should not be confused with the current conception of nation-building. In terms of this case study, the Philippines more accurately represented an example of indigenous nation-building with American support. The Americans involved in the counterinsurgency campaign in the Philippines understood that the situation could not be solved by military assistance alone. Reform and change was necessary throughout the government, and that required significant financial aid and almost intimate advisory support.

The Huk campaign clearly highlights the importance of security sector reform. However, US officials from both the Department of State and Defense tended to default to the importance of the material aid provided to the Philippines. The embassy's *chargé de affairs*, while noting the need for the right personnel in the Philippines, then focused on the type of equipment the US was providing the AFP. JUSMAG officials then echoed this preoccupation with material assistance by correlating improved *esprit de corps* within the AFP to the delivery of US weapons and equipment.[19] Lansdale appreciated the difference between material aid and the aid he provided. "If we understand that this is war over people, then we can start understanding the real human values in it - which go far beyond sizes of forces, reports of battles, statistics on casualties, [and] differences in quality [of] weapons."[20]

The US government did not benefit from its long association with the Philippines and the inherent understanding that should have accompanied that association. This meant officials involved in the campaign could not remain passive in their approach. It is perhaps necessary to heed the warning of the noted military theorist Sir B. H. Liddell Hart that "those who frame policy and apply it need a better understanding of the subject [support for guerrilla warfare] than has been shown in the past."[21] While his caution referenced Allied support for partisan and guerrilla organizations during World War II and the potentially long-term, detrimental effects that type of warfare had on society, it still has bearing on this subject. By suggesting that previous policy-makers did not spend enough time understanding the moral and ethical implications of unleashing an irregular form of warfare, he implied a basic need for historical understanding prior to developing and implementing policy.

Lansdale grasped his own shortcomings in this field. In 1948 he requested assistance from the Department of the Army Public Information Office in procuring any historical material they could find on guerrilla warfare and insurgency going "back to biblical times, if necessary."[22] Unfortunately, it is unclear whether other American personnel in the Philippines were as proactive as Lansdale in trying to grasp the complexities of the problems facing the country.

Choosing the proper personnel to assist in an intervention in a foreign country is another important lesson from the Huk campaign. Embassy officials in the Philippines understood they needed individuals knowledgeable in counterinsurgency operations. Once those individuals are in place they must be afforded the opportunity to complete the mission, unhindered by administrative or bureaucratic requirements. Lansdale was in the Philippines for around six and a half years from mid-1945 to early-1954. During that time he was able to develop relationships that facilitated his covert operations in the Philippines. The effect of Lansdale's departure was indirectly noted by members of the intelligence community. "The [State Department] despatches that came in and described what was happening were of much more value than the spot reports that came from the CIA . . . I don't think they knew a great deal about Philippine political history."[23]

Frequent personnel turnover hinders the development of institutional knowledge and locally based contact networks and is not lost on host nation nationals. The editor of the Manila Chronicle, Ernie del Rosario once told an embassy official:

> You know, Jim, there's one problem with Americans that come out here in the embassy and the military and they come to negotiate. They forget that Filipinos know a great deal more about Americans than Americans know about Filipinos. They come here and they stay here for a couple of years, two or three, and then they go off and they leave.[24]

The Huk campaign case study demonstrates the significant benefits of employing personnel with deep host nation sociocultural understanding. As one embassy official recollects, "There was a certain amount of self-delusion in our reporting…we could never really assess because we weren't around long enough to see the ultimate effects."[25] It also highlights the drawbacks of personnel who presume that major, life altering events such as World War II, have not altered the status quo in some way. Additionally, individuals who assumed their experience in other Asian nations qualified them as experts in Philippine affairs without additional study and experience, only distracted from rather than added to the solution.

The right personnel would be useless without clearly defined objectives from policy makers. Lansdale departed Washington for the Philippines with defined, realistic objectives, *only after* Ramon Magsaysay emerged from the chaotic Philippine political scene. As mentioned earlier, the Americans understood that change and reform were necessary throughout the Philippine government. They also understood that change and reform had to come from within, and overt US pressure and influence would ultimately undermine their regional policy objectives.

The emergence of Magsaysay reflects the need for partners of character and integrity who are committed to their own ideals rather than ideals they think are important to Americans. Magsaysay's ideals and vision coincided and corresponded with American ideals and objectives, making him an ideal partner. Magsaysay was not simply an American puppet. He maintained his own ideals, at times butting heads with American officials.[26] An indigenous official committed to his or her own ideals and beliefs is more likely to come across as genuine and find it easier to deflect criticism or accusations of undue external influence. Magsaysay's personality and character also lent significantly to success in the Philippines. "Ed Lansdale was obviously his tactician but Magsaysay understood Filipinos very well and he knew how to reach them. They made a great team."[27] Selecting the right partner was a matter of understanding the nature of the problem in the Philippines and identifying an individual capable of positively influencing the situation, in this case, popular faith and trust in the government.

The Huk campaign was characterized by almost unprecedented unity of effort within the US team in the Philippines. The "country team" concept originated during the period of the Huk campaign though it is unclear if Lansdale's claim, that the country team concept was the brainchild of Counselor of Embassy William Lacy, is factual.[28] Other than a negative relationship with one JUSMAG chief, Major General Pierson, it appears that Lansdale had a very good relationship with the other JUSMAG chiefs of the period, notably generals Hobbs and Cannon.[29] He also had very strong relationships with ambassadors Myron Cowen and Raymond Spruance, and Counselor of Embassy William Lacy. The team in the Philippines relied on personal relationships built on trust and mutual support. Lansdale's authority afforded him the power to demand support, but he preferred instead to build supportive relationships within the embassy team.

Another important lesson from the Huk campaign is the level of Filipino involvement in US plans and operations in the Philippines. Lansdale's covert operations directly and indirectly incorporated support, input, and actions from the Filipinos.[30] He understood that they were all working towards a common goal, and no one was more invested in the successful outcome of American operations in the Philippines than Filipinos themselves.[31] Many Americans abroad displayed a certain degree of arrogance in their actions.[32] Lansdale and his team eschewed that way of operating and sought local help in developing solutions to problems. In his opinion,

> If we move in on a foreign people to help them, and see this only as a pragmatic exercise, equating full bellies with man's liberty, or compromise our principles in the name of expediency, or let the egos of some turn Americans into big frogs in little ponds, then we can stifle that very, precious spark of true national life we seek to help protect and guide towards strength.[33]

By working with and through Filipino counterparts who were fully invested in and believed in the mission, the entire Philippine-American team benefited.

The counterinsurgent leadership in the Philippines, both Filipino and American, understood the importance of security sector reform. Rather than focusing on a materiel and increasing end strength, they opted instead to focus on professionalizing the existing security forces.[34] The key aspect of Magsaysay's military reforms was the priority given to rebuilding the morale and professionalism of the Philippine military throughout the chain of command. This was largely accomplished first through Magsaysay's ability to promote, demote, and fire officers, regardless of rank or political association. In a military characterized by a politicized officer corps, the senior security sector official had to have the ability to rid the organization of negative influences without political interference. Magsaysay's empathy for his soldiers led to the next key factor in professionalizing the security forces. By acknowledging and remedying the underlying causes of his soldier's poor treatment of the populace he successfully prevented further abuses and revitalized the military's relationship with the people.

As mentioned in the previous section, Lansdale attempted to export his experiences in the Philippines to his later operations in Vietnam and experienced far different results. Any successful counterinsurgency practitioner risks falling victim to similar mistakes when asked to develop and execute a counterinsurgency campaign in another place at another time. The enduring lesson from Lansdale's dual experiences is that in another place and another time, context has changed. In the Philippines Lansdale had significant freedom of movement, allowing him to see the context of the problem firsthand. From his earliest days in Vietnam, Lansdale's reputation preceded him, preventing him from developing the same kind of understanding he developed in the Philippines, perhaps preventing him from understanding the nature of the problem.[35]

The final enduring lesson from the Huk campaign lies in the available history of the campaign itself. Militarily, the vast majority of the existing scholarship focuses almost solely on Lansdale and Magsaysay's efforts to defeat the Huks. Politically, the scholarship focuses on US diplomatic and Philippine government actions to counter the communists. Many of the conclusions derived from the existing scholarship subsequently emphasize the US and Philippine military, governmental, and diplomatic effects on the PKP-Huk movement, with little acknowledgment of their internal divisions and conflicts. Absent the work of largely one individual, Dr. Benedict Kerkvliet, there would be little understanding of the internal conflict within the PKP-Huk movement. Failure to acknowledge the nuances of an opponent's weaknesses lends to substantially flawed understanding of the true historical sequence of events, and tends to promote a one-sided, egotistical account of events.

The Huk campaign provides an excellent case study of a successful, limited intervention counterinsurgency campaign. In less than four years the insurgency ceased to be an existential threat to the government, popular faith in government was restored, and government institutions and processes were reformed and strengthened. Ramon Magsaysay and Edward Lansdale formed the nucleus of a team that achieved significant victories over both the Huks and negative forces within the Philippine government itself. The enduring lessons from the campaign suggest that while it is impossible to duplicate the conditions of the Huk campaign, it may be possible to replicate them.

Notes

1. B. H. Liddell Hart, *Strategy* (New York: Frederick A. Praeger, 1967), 380-381.

2. Ramon Magsaysay, Jr., interview with the author, Pasay City, Manila, 22 October 2012.

3. Napoleon Valeriano, "Colonel Valeriano's Speech," Given at unknown location or date (Lansdale Papers, Box 15, Hoover Institution Archives, Stanford University, Palo Alto, CA), 6.

4. Ramon Magsaysay, Jr., interview with the author, Pasay City, Manila, 22 October 2012.

5. Alfredo Lim, interview with the author, Manila City Hall, 22 October 2012.

6. Karnow, 702.

7. Lorenzo Tanada, Untitled Speech, Rotary Club, Baguio, Philippines, March 1947 (Lansdale Papers, Box 32, Hoover Institution Archives, Stanford University, Palo Alto, CA).

8. Steinberg, 185.

9. Frisco San Juan, interview with the author, Quezon City, Manila, 15 October 2012.

10. Romulo, Gray, 13-14; Taruc, *Born of the People*, 13.

11. Romulo, Gray, 37, 41; Taruc, *Born of the People*, 35-36.

12. Romulo, Gray, 39-40; Taruc, *Born of the People*, 18-19, 22-24.

13. Romulo, Gray, 47, 72-73, 99-100, 139-140; Taruc, *He Who Rides the Tiger*, 86.

14. Isaacs, "The Danger in the Philippines, Part 2." See also Romulo, Gray, 267, and Taruc, *He Who Rides the Tiger*, 80-84.

15. Arlington National Cemetery, http://www.arlingtoncemetery.net/ apierson.htm, (accessed 27 November 2012). For the 11th Airborne Division's relationship with the Huks, see Taruc, *Born of the People*, 199.

16. Pierson was stationed in the Philippines starting in 1936, a period when MacArthur was arguably one of the most important Americans in the Philippines. As a general officer during operations in New Guinea, the Philippines, and with occupation forces in Japan, Pierson may have been significantly influenced by MacArthur. MacArthur was known for his dislike of the OSS and organizations he could not control. If Pierson was a MacArthur adherent, that might explain his dislike of Lansdale and his mission in the Philippines.

17. James J. Halsema interview.

18. Cliff Forster interview.

19. The Ambassador in the Philippines (Cowen) to the Secretary of State, 25 October 1951, *Foreign Relations of the United States*, 1951, 6, p. 1574.

20. Edward Lansdale, "Symposium on The Challenge of Subversive Insurgency," lecture, Michigan State University, Lansing, MI, 29 February 1964, (Lansdale Papers, Box 74, Hoover Institution Archives, Stanford University, Palo Alto, CA).

21. Hart, *Strategy*, 382.

22. Memorandum to Public Information Division, Department of the Army, *Information about Guerrillas*, 27 April 1948 (Lansdale Papers, Box 33, Hoover Institution Archives, Stanford University, Palo Alto, CA).

23. Stephen Low interview.

24. James T. Pettus, Jr., Press Attaché, USIS, Manila (1954-1957); interviewed by G. Lewis Schmidt (30 May 1990), ADST/CRS.

25. James J. Halsema interview.

26. Ramon Magsaysay, Jr., interview with the author, Pasay City, Manila, 22 October 2012. In one instance, Magsaysay informed embassy officials they had to find a new bombing range for Clark Air Base because of complaints he received from farmers in the area surrounding the existing bombing range.

27. James J. Halsema interview.

28. Lansdale, *In the Midst of Wars*, 114. The first move towards the country team was actually enacted by President Truman through Executive Order no. 10338, which was approved by Congress on 10 October 1951. The Department of State describes the country team as consisting of "all Embassy sections and heads the heads of each [US government] agency at post," where "each member reports to the Ambassador on activities, next steps for their office. The Ambassador resolves differences, if any, and seeks guidance from Washington if course corrections appear necessary." The team then "formulates the Mission Strategic Plan that spells out specific, details [US government] interaction in that country" (US Department of State, "Introduction to Department of State Agency Culture," http://www.state.gov/courses/rs401/page_25.htm, accessed on 3 December 2012).

29. Director of Central Intelligence Walter B. Smith to Major General Leland Hobbs, personal correspondence, 9 January 1951 (Lansdale Papers, Box 34, Hoover Institution Archives, Stanford University, Palo Alto, CA). After the conclusion of Lansdale's initial assignment in the Philippines, Hobbs actively sought approval from the Director of Central Intelligence for an extension of Lansdale's tour. In a handwritten note at the bottom of the letter, the Director Smith wrote "I agree with you. He is almost indispensable where he is." For Lansdale's assessment of Major General Cannon see Lansdale, *The Philippines Election, 1953*, 2.

30. Edward Lansdale, *Memorandum for Matt Baird*, 1 March 1961 (Lansdale Papers, Box 97, Hoover Institution Archives, Stanford University, Palo Alto, CA). In this memorandum, Lansdale specifically cites individual AFP officers who made all of their main programs and initiatives "click."

31. Lansdale, "Lessons Learned, The Philippines: 1946-1953," Interdepartmental Course on Counterinsurgency.

32. Robert L. Nichols interview.

33. Lansdale, "Lessons Learned, The Philippines: 1946-1953," Interdepartmental Course on Counterinsurgency.

34. This decision was aided by the fact that the US was the guarantor of Philippine sovereignty and defense from external threats, minimizing the need for a large, conventionally trained military that organizationally mirrored its American counterpart.

35. Currey, 128.

Appendix A
Map of Primary Huk Influence

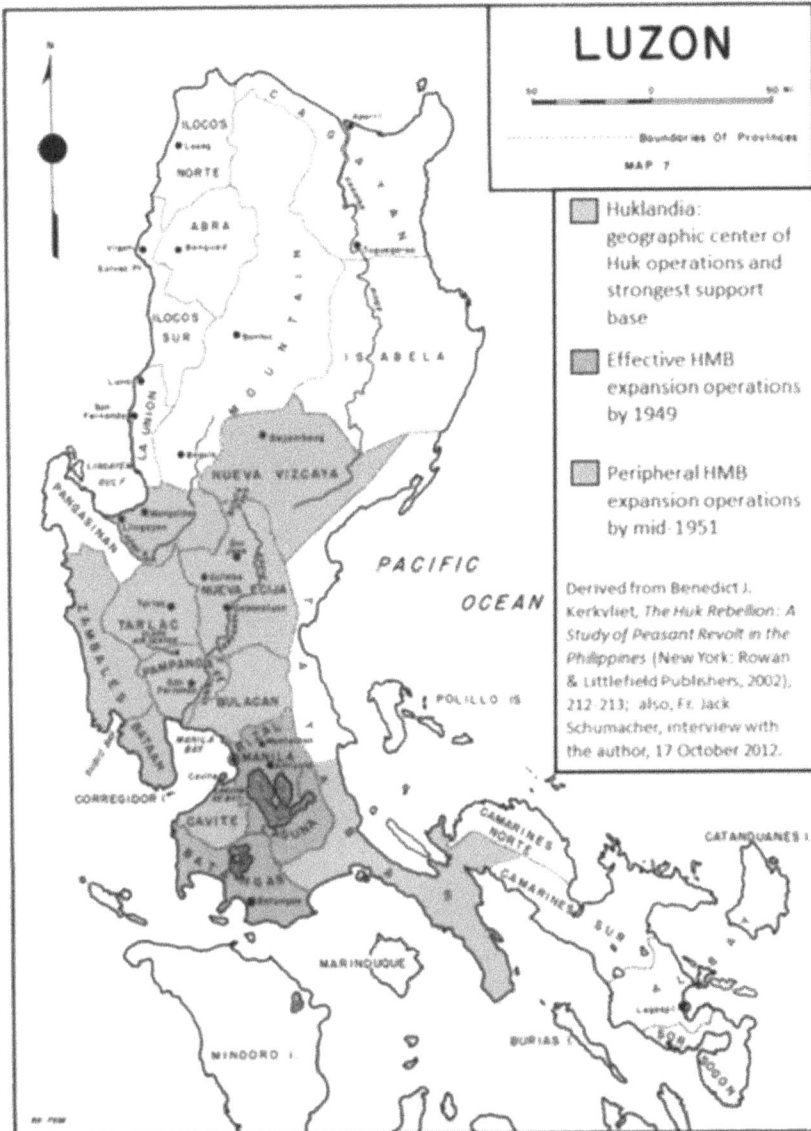

Map created by the author utilizing a base map courtesy of: http://www.ibiblio.org/
hyperwar/USMC/USMC-M-AvPhil/USMC-M-AvPhil-3.html.

Appendix B
Subject Biographical Timelines

Edward G. Lansdale

1942 Begins working for OSS as a civilian

February, 1943 Reappointed to the Army with the Military Intelligence Service in San Francisco

October, 1945 Assigned to G2, Philippines Ryuku Command (PHILRYCOM), based in Manila

June, 1947 Takes over duties as PHILRYCOM Public Information Officer

November, 1948 Departs Manila

February, 1949 Assigned to Lowry AFB, Colorado as an instructor

November, 1949 Reassigned to the Central Control Group, Office of Policy Coordination, Washington, DC

Early, 1950 Meets Magsaysay for the first time in Washington, DC

September, 1950 Returns to the Philippines, with a cover as Intelligence Advisor to Filipino president Elpidio Quirino

June, 1952 Accompanies Magsaysay to International Lions Club convention in Mexico City

March, 1953 Reassigned to 13th Air Force historical division at Clark Air Base after fallout with MG Pierson

June, 1953 Travels with General Michael O'Daniel's military mission to Vietnam

July, 1953 Returns from Vietnam

November, 1953 Magsaysay elected president

January, 1954 Departs the Philippines for last time

Ramon Magsaysay

April, 1942 Joins COL Gyles Merrill's guerrillas in Zambales Province

February, 1945 Selected as Military Governor of Zambales

April, 1946 Elected to House of Representatives for Zambales

1946 Becomes Chairman of the House National Defense Committee

November, 1949 Reelected to House of Representatives for Zambales

Early, 1950 Visits Washington, DC with congressional delegation, meets Lansdale for the first time

August, 1950 Appointed Secretary of National Defense by President Elpidio Quirino

September, 1950 Moves into Lansdale's quarters on Camp Murphy

June, 1952 Keynote speaker at the International Lions Club convention in Mexico City

1952 Huks launch retaliatory attack on his home town

February, 1953 Resigns as Secretary of National Defense after President Quirino makes disparaging comments to the press

April, 1953 Candidacy for president announced at the Nacionalista Party convention

November, 1953 Elected President of the Philippine Republic

December, 1953 Inauguration

May, 1954 Luis Taruc surrenders to the Philippine government

Appendix C
Interviewee Biographical Data

Fidel V. Ramos

President Ramos served as the 12th President of the Republic of the Philippines from 1992-1998. He also served as Chief of the Philippine Constabulary, Chief of Staff of the Armed Forces of the Philippines, Chief of Staff of the Integrated National Police, and Secretary of National Defense.

President Ramos graduated from the United States Military Academy at West Point in 1950 and served in the Philippine Army during the Huk campaign as a lieutenant and captain. He also served with the 20th BCT during its deployment to fight in the Korean War. In 1962 he became the Group Commander for the 1st Special Forces Group (Airborne), Philippine Army. In 1966 he deployed to Vietnam as the Chief of Staff of the 1st Philippine Civic Action Group.

Ramon B. Magsaysay, Jr.

Senator Magsaysay served two terms in the Philippine Senate from 1995-2007, having started his political career in 1966 as the congressman for Zambales Province. Senator Magsaysay studied at the Harvard Business School and New York University Business School in the early 1960s. In the 1970s he became a successful businessman in the Philippine telecommunications industry.

Senator Magsaysay is the son of former president Ramon Magsaysay, Sr., and was a teenager at the time of his father's election to the presidency.

Alfredo S. Lim

Mr. Lim is currently serving his fourth term as Mayor of Manila, the first three terms being 1992-1995, 1995-1998, and 2007-2010. He holds bachelor's degrees in Business Administration and Law from the University of the East, and a master's degree in National Security Administration from the National Defense College of the Philippines.

As the Manila Chief of Police in the 1980s, Lim led the police force in retaking government installations from rebellious military units during the 1987 attempted coup. Under President Corazon Aquino's administration Lim was appointed Director of the National Bureau of Investigation. During the early 1950s Mr. Lim was a member of the Manila police force.

Frisco F. San Juan

Mr. San Juan served two congressional terms from 1966-1973. Amongst his many committee memberships, Mr. San Juan served on the Committee on National Security and Defense and Peace and Order, and was Chairman of the Sub-Committee on Veterans Affairs. He is currently the president of the Nationalist People's Coalition, a Philippine political party.

During World War II Mr. Lim served with Hunters ROTC Guerrillas. Following the war he was a National Commander of the Philippine Veterans Legion. Mr. San Juan served on the personal staff of Ramon Magsaysay during his tenure as Secretary of National Defense, and later as chief of Magsaysay's inner cordon security element. He was a founding member of NAMFREL, and was intimately involved in the counterinsurgency campaign against the Huks. He would later go on to be one of the founding members of the Freedom Company, an organization that aided in Lansdale's covert operations in Vietnam.

Romeo B. Taruc

Dr. Taruc is a physician and former city councilor for Angeles City, Pampanga. He continues to play an active role in local politics in his home province of Pampanga, and is on the board of directors of the Philippine Land Bank.

Dr. Taruc is the only son of former Huk supreme military commander Luis Taruc. During parts of the Huk campaign, Dr. Taruc traveled with his father and was directly involved in his father's negotiations with President Quirino in 1953.

John N. Schumacher

Father Schumacher is a retired Jesuit priest and historian. He is a recipient of Ateneo University's Lifetime Achievement Award, and is the author of *Father Jose Burgos: Priest and Nationalist* (Manila: Ateneo University, 1972). He was first posted to the Philippines in 1948 to study at the seminary in Novaliches, Quezon City. From 1951-1954 Father Schumacher taught high school seminary in Quezon City.

Bibliography

Government Documents

A Report to the National Security Council by the Executive Security on United States Objectives and Programs for National Security (NSC-68). Washington, DC: Government Printing Office, 1950.

Bureau of Political-Military Affairs. *US Government Counterinsurgency Guide*. Washington, DC: Government Printing Office, 2009.

Central Intelligence Agency. "Freedom of Information Act." Central Intelligence Agency Electronic Reading Room. http://www.foia.cia.gov/search.asp (accessed 27 August 2012).

Economic Survey Mission to the Philippines. *Report to the President of the United States by the Economic Survey Mission to the Philippines.* Washington, DC: Government Printing Office, 1950.

Executive Order no. 10338. *Coordination Procedures under Section 507 of the Mutual Security Act of 1951.* http://trumanlibrary.org/executiveorders/index.php?pid=178 (accessed 20 August 2012).

General Headquarters, Far East Command. *A Brief History of the G-2 Section, GHQ, SWPA (Southwest Pacific Area) and Affiliated Units.* Tokyo: Government Printing Office, 1948.

General Headquarters, United States Army Forces, Pacific, Military Intelligence Section, General Staff. *Intelligence Activities in the Philippines During the Japanese Occupation.* Tokyo: Government Printing Office, 1948.

Greenberg, Lawrence M. *The Hukbalahap Insurrection: A Case Study of a Successful Anti-Insurgency Operation in the Philippines, 1946-1955.* Analysis Branch, US Army Center of Military History. Washington, DC: Government Printing Office, 1986.

United Kingdom, Ministry of Defense. *Army Field Manual: Countering Insurgency*, vol. 1, part 10, January 2010.

US Department of the Army. *Field Manual 3-24: Counterinsurgency.* Washington, DC: Government Printing Office, 2006.

US Department of the Army. *Field Manual 3-24.2: Tactics in Counterinsurgency.* Washington, DC: Government Printing Office, 2008.

US Department of State. *Foreign Relations of the United States, 1946*, Vol. 3: The Far East. Washington, DC: Government Printing Office, 1971.

US Department of State. *Foreign Relations of the United States, 1947*, Vol. 6: The Far East. Washington, DC: Government Printing Office, 1972.

US Department of State. *Foreign Relations of the United States, 1948*, Vol. 6: The Far East and Australia. Washington, DC: Government Printing Office, 1974.

US Department of State. *Foreign Relations of the United States, 1949*, Vol. 7: The Far East and Australia, Part 1. Washington, DC: Government Printing Office, 1975.

US Department of State. *Foreign Relations of the United States, 1950*, Vol. 6: East Asia and the Pacific. Washington, DC: Government Printing Office, 1976.

US Department of State. *Foreign Relations of the United States, 1951*, Vol. 6: Asia and the Pacific. Washington, DC: Government Printing Office, 1977.

US Department of State. *Foreign Relations of the United States, 1952-1954*, Vol. 12: East Asia and the Pacific. Washington, DC: Government Printing Office, 1987.

Archives

Charles T. R. Bohannon Papers, 1915-1985. The Hoover Institution Library and Archives, Stanford University, CA.

Edward Geary Lansdale Papers, 1910-1987. The Hoover Institution Library and Archives, Stanford University, CA.

Myron M. Cowen Papers, 1948-1965. Harry S. Truman Library and Museum, Independence, MO.

Association for Diplomatic Studies and Training, Oral History Country Reader Series, Philippines, http://adst.org/oral-history/country-reader-series/ (accessed 25 October 2012).

Interviews

Lim, Alfredo. Manila City Hall, Manila, 22 October 2012.

Magsaysay, Ramon, Jr. Manila, 22 October 2012.

Ramos, Fidel V. Makati City, Manila, 22 October 2012.

San Juan, Frisco. Quezon City, Manila, 15 October 2012.

Schumacher, Jack. Jesuit Residence, Ateneo University, Manila, 17 October 2012.

Taruc, Romeo. Angeles City, Pampanga, 18 October 2012.

Books

Aldrich, Richard J., Gary D. Rawnsley, and Ming-Yeh T. Rawnsley, ed. *The Clandestine Cold War in Asia, 1945-65: Western Intelligence, Propaganda and Special Operations.* London: Frank Cass, 2000.

Averch, H. A., F. H. Denton, and J. E. Koehler. *A Crisis of Ambiguity: Political and Economic Development in the Philippines*, a report prepared for Agency for International Development. Santa Monica, CA: RAND, 1970.

Baclagon, Uldarico S. *Lessons from the Huk Campaign in the Philippines.* Manila: M. Colcol & Company, 1956.

Buell, Thomas B. *The Quiet Warrior: A Biography of Admiral Raymond A. Spruance.* Annapolis, MD: Naval Institute Press, 1987.

Currey, Cecil B. *Edward Lansdale: The Unquiet American.* Washington: Brassey's, 1998.

Guardia, Michael. *American Guerrilla: The Forgotten Heroics of Russell W. Volckmann.* Havertown, PA: Casemate Publishers, 2010.

Hart, B. H. Liddell. *Strategy.* New York: Frederick A. Praeger, 1967.

Hickey, Gerald C., John L. Wilkinson. *Agrarian Reform in the Philippines: Report of a Seminar*, December 16-17, 1977 at the Rand Corporation, Washington, DC

Hunt, Ray C., and Bernard Norling. *Behind Japanese Lines: An American Guerrilla in the Philippines.* Lexington, KY: University Press of Kentucky, 1986.

Karnow, Stanley. *In Our Image: America's Empire in the Philippines.* New York: Ballantine Books, 1989. Google e-book.

Kerkvliet, Benedict J. *The Huk Rebellion: A Study of Peasant Revolt in the Philippines.* New York: Rowman & Littlefield Publishers, Inc., 2002.

Lansdale, Edward G. *In the Midst of Wars.* New York: Harper & Row, Publishers, 1972.

Macdonald, Douglas J. *Adventures in Chaos: American Intervention for Reform in the Third World.* Cambridge: Harvard University Press, 1992.

Manchester, William. *American Caesar.* New York: Hachette Book Group, 1978. Google e-book.

Marston, Daniel. *Rock in an Angry Sea: The Indian Army 1945-1947.* Cambridge: Cambridge University Press, 2013.

Marston, Daniel, and Carter Malkasian, ed. *Counterinsurgency in Modern Warfare*. Oxford: Osprey Publishing, 2008.

Niehoff, Arthur H., ed. *A Casebook of Social Change*. Chicago: Aldine Publishing Company, 1966.

Pomeroy, William J. *Guerrilla and Counter-Guerrilla Warfare: Liberation and Suppression in the Present Period*. New York: International Publishers, 1964.

———. *The Forest*. New York: International Publishers, 1963.

Putzel, James. *A Captive Land: The Politics of Agrarian Reforms in the Philippines*. London: Catholic Institute for International Relations, 1992.

Recto, Claro M. *Three Years of Enemy Occupation*. Manila: Cacho Hermanos, 1973. Reprint of Manila: People's Publishers, 1946.

Romulo, Carlos P. *Crusade in Asia: Philippine Victory*. New York: The John Day Company, 1955.

Romulo, Carlos P., Marvin M. Gray. *The Magsaysay Story*. New York: The John Day Company, 1956.

Seeman, Bernard, and Laurence Salisbury. *Cross-Currents in the Philippines* (New York: Institute of Pacific Relations, 1946).

Taruc, Luis. *Born of the People*. New York: International Publishers, 1953.

———. *He Who Rides the Tiger*. New York: Frederick A. Praeger, 1967.

Valeriano, Napoleon D., Charles T.R. Bohannon. *Counter-Guerrilla Operations: The Philippine Experience*. Westport, CT: Praeger Security International, 1962, 2006.

Journals and Periodicals

Appleton, Sheldon. "Communism and the Chinese in the Philippines." *Pacific Affairs* 32, no. 4 (December 1959): 376-391.

Bungaard, Leslie R. "Philippine Local Government." *The Journal of Politics* 19, no. 2 (May 1957): 262-283.

Chapman, Abraham. "Note on the Philippine Elections." *Pacific Affairs* 19, no. 2 (June 1946): 193-198.

Choi, Jaepil. "A Motivational Theory of Charismatic Leadership: Envisioning, Empathy, and Empowerment." *Journal of Leadership and Organizational Studies* 13, no. 1 (2006): 24-43.

del Castillo, Mateo, Luis M. Taruc, and Manuel Roxas. "Taruc-Roxas Correspondence." *Far Eastern Survey* 15, no. 20 (9 October 1946): 314-317.

Emerson, Rupert. "The Erosion of Democracy." *The Journal of Asian Studies* 20, no. 1 (November 1960): 1-8.

Entenberg, Barbara. "Agrarian Reform and the Hukbalahap." *Far Eastern Survey* 15, no. 16 (14 August 1946): 245-248.

Fifield, Russell H. "Philippine Foreign Policy." *Far Eastern Survey* 20, no. 4 (21 February 1951): 33-38.

———. "The Hukbalahap Today." *Far Eastern Survey* 20, no. 2 (24 January 1951): 13-18.

Finkelstein, Lawrence S. "US at Impasse in Southeast Asia." *Far Eastern Survey* 19, no. 16 (27 September 1950): 165-172.

Gosnell, Harold F. "An Interpretation of the Philippine Election of 1953." The American Political Science Review 48, no. 4 (December 1954): 1128-1138.

Halsema, James J. "Development Plans in the Philippines." *Far Eastern Survey* 18, no. 20 (5 October 1949): 233-239.

Hart, Donn V. "Magsaysay: Philippine Candidate." *Far Eastern Survey* 22, no. 6 (May 1953): 67-70.

———. "The Philippine Cooperative Movement." *Far Eastern Survey* 24, no. 2 (February 1955): 27-30.

Jenkins, Shirley. "Great Expectations in the Philippines." *Far Eastern Survey* 16, no. 15 (13 August 1947): 169-174.

———. "Philippine White Paper." *Far Eastern Survey* 20, no. 1 (10 January 1951): 1-6.

Klatt, W. "Agrarian Issues in Asia: II. Reform and Insurgency." *International Affairs (Royal Institute of International Affairs 1944-)* 48, no. 3 (July 1972): 395-413.

Lande, Carl H. "Parties and Politics in the Philippines." *Asian Survey* 8, no. 9 (September 1968): 725-747.

Lansang, Jose A. "The Philippine-American Experiment: A Filipino View." *Pacific Affairs* 25, no. 3 (September 1952): 226-234.

Machado, K. G. "From Traditional Faction to Machine: Changing

Patterns of Political Leadership and Organization in the Rural Philippines." *The Journal of Asian Studies* 33, no. 4 (August 1974): 523-547.

McHale, Thomas R. "Problems of Economic Development in the Philippines." *Pacific Affairs* 25, no. 2 (June 1952): 160-169.

Roces, Mina. "Kinship Politics in Post-War Philippines: The Lopes Family. 1945-1989." *Modern Asian Studies* 34, no. 1 (February 2000): 181-221.

Romani, John H. "The Philippine Barrio." *Far Eastern Quarterly* 15, no. 2 (February 1956): 229-237.

Satoshi, Nakano. "Gabriel L. Kaplan and US Involvement in Philippine Electoral Democracy: A Tale of Two Democracies." *Philippine Studies* 52, no. 2 (2004): 149-178.

Scott, James C. "Patron-Client Politics and Political Change in Southeast Asia." *The American Political Science Review* 66, no. 1 (March 1972): 91-113.

Starner, Frances L. "Philippine Economic Development and the Two-Party System." *Asian Survey* 2, no. 5 (July 1962): 17-23.

Steinberg, David J. "An Ambiguous Legacy: Years at War in the Philippines." *Pacific Affairs* 45, no. 2 (Summer 1972): 165-190.

Stephens, Robert P. "The Prospect of Social Progress in the Philippines." *Pacific Affairs* 23, no. 2 (June 1950): 139-152.

Sturtevant, David R. "Sakdalism and Philippine Radicalism." *The Journal of Asian Studies* 21, no. 2 (February 1962): 199-213.

van den Muijzenberg, Otto. "Political Mobilization and Violence in Central Luzon (Philippines)." *Modern Asian Studies* 7, no. 4 (1973): 691-705.

van der Kroef, Justus M. "Communism and Reform in the Philippines." *Pacific Affairs* 46, no. 1 (Spring, 1973): 29-58.

———. "Philippine Communism and the Chinese." *The China Quarterly*, no. 30 (April-June 1967): 115-148.

Vinacke, Harold M. "Post-War Government and Politics of the Philippines." *The Journal of Politics* 9, no. 4 (November 1947): 717-730.

Wurfel, David. "Philippine Agrarian Reform under Magsaysay, Part 2." *Far Eastern Survey* 27, no. 2 (February 1958): 23-30.

Additional Resources

Catapusan, Benicio T. "Agrarian Conflicts as the Bases for Agrarian Legislation." United States Agency for International Development, http://pdf.usaid.gov/pdf_docs/ PNABH968.pdf (accessed 14 July 2012).

Gentry, William A., Todd J. Webber, and Golnaz Sadri, *Empathy in the Workplace: A Tool for Effective Leadership*. Greensboro, NC: Center for Creative Leadership, 2010.

Greenberg, David R. "The US Response to Philippine Insurgency." PhD diss., Tufts University, The Fletcher School of Law and Diplomacy, 1994.

www.ingramcontent.com/pod-product-compliance
Lightning Source LLC
Chambersburg PA
CBHW081418090426
42738CB00017B/3408